Additional photography by Nicho Troup

CHUPI PUBLISHING

*For my mother Veronica who inspired and taught
me how to cook with the freshest home
grown vegetables.*

Chupi Publishing
2 North Parade Passage
Bath
BA1 1NX

Green World Cooking

Printed by Scotprint, East Lothian, Scotland
Printed with soya based inks on 50% recycled paper, sourced from
sustainable forest, totally chlorine free (TCF)

ISBN 0 9531119 1 1

Bibliography

International Dictionary of Food and Cooking by Charles Sinclair, published 1998 by Peter
Collin Publishing Ltd.

The Oxford Companion to Food by Alan Davidson, published 1999 by Oxford University Press.

CONTENTS

INTRODUCTION

The recipes in this book are but a small part of the large number that my partner Nicho and I have eaten, enjoyed and collected, from our years of travelling the world together. We've included a few pictures from those travels as well.

The recipes have all been cooked in Demuths Restaurant in Bath and have been enjoyed by the hundreds of thousands of you who have supported us in the 15 years since we opened, and have enabled Demuths to evolve into one of the most successful vegetarian restaurants in Britain today.

They have been tweaked, changed and adapted by those wonderful people who have worked with us and whose input has given us the energy and inspiration to carry on.

This is not posh food. It's unpretentious, to be served on any occasion. The ingredients seldom need to be fancy, they should, however, be fresh and of good quality, for even the best of cooks can't make a delicious meal out of poor ingredients.

Whilst nearly all the ingredients can be bought from supermarkets, some can only be obtained from specialist shops. If there are locally farmed alternatives then do go for them, for though probably dirtier, in return they will be fresher and cheaper. Frequent your farm shop, farmers market and wholefood shop, whenever and wherever you can.

Try to eat seasonally. Don't be seduced by supermarkets offering you vegetables and fruit out of season, for example, asparagus and strawberries in mid-winter, it's normally not what you need at that time of year. Your body, if you listen to it, will choose the right food for the right season. In winter we are drawn to filling, robust root vegetables and in summer to light, bright salad type food.

If you have the choice and can afford it then buy organic, as fruit and vegetables produced in this way are pesticide, herbicide and additive free. Buying organic is one way to ensure that future generations have a chance to inherit naturally abundant unpolluted land.

We at Demuths are totally against the use of any ingredients that contain any material derived from genetically modified origins – GMO's. Aside from the potential health issues, which are not conclusively proven one way or the other, small farmers in developing countries cannot afford to be tied to multinational seed companies and should be free to produce, trade and barter their own seed.

Again if you have the choice, buy fairly traded produce as it must be better to guarantee a fair wage to those who live and work in those countries where wages and working conditions are traditionally poor. We have so much to learn from countries which may not have our level of affluence, but have much more to offer in their holistic approach to farming and food, where meals are prepared and shared as a major part of family and cultural life, unlike us where the takeaway television lifestyle is now the norm.

In many societies recipes are never written down, just handed down from parent to child. In India part of a dowry will be an unwritten repertoire of the bride's family recipes, learned by watching parents and grandparents. In this way culinary traditions are passed from generation to generation. There are no precise measurements, just a handful of this and a pinch of that. The best way to learn to cook is by watching, by trial and error, by feeling the texture with your hands, and most importantly by tasting as you go along.

What fascinates me about cooking is that however slavishly recipes are followed, the results are always different, because we ourselves are all different. Of course it can depend on equipment, ovens and temperature but especially on the mood of the cook.

For me the single most important element in successful cooking is to put as much love and care into its preparation as possible. I believe that food made with love always tastes far better and is more satisfying and nourishing.

Just remember cooking should be fun.

Rachel

STARTERS

Short Eats

Small and easy to make dishes, for any time of day

Soups

Soups that are almost a meal in themselves

Short Eats

The term 'short eats' was originally used in Sri Lanka in colonial times, to describe small dishes that accompanied drinks. Most countries have their short eats.

The Spanish have tapas which comes from the word for 'cover'. They were originally slices of bread placed over a sherry glass to keep flies out. The French hors-d'oeuvres are snacks or dishes served at the beginning of a meal, and the Italian antipasto is the first course of a meal.

Middle Eastern mezze comes from the Iranian word 'maza', meaning to taste or relish. They were traditionally eaten with wine, but are now eaten with mint tea. In Russia zakuski, which are 'little bites', are eaten with vodka to cleanse the palate between each bite. Further east, from India to South East Asia, snacks are eaten on the street at any time of day; often fried, hot and spicy, always moreish.

These short eats can be served as an appetiser and most can be eaten with the fingers. The chief requisite of 'short eats' is that they should be very tasty and appeal to the eye as well as the palate.

There is nothing better than sharing different 'short eats' over a glass of wine.

Baked haloumi, with its chewy and salty taste, leaves you wanting more and contrasts wonderfully with the cherry tomatoes and the sweetness of the roasted peppers.

Haloumi, Tomato and Pepper Brochettes
with Balsamic Drizzle and Curly Endive

SERVES 4

250 g haloumi, cut into 16 cubes

2 tbsps olive oil

1 red pepper, cut into 8 chunks

1 yellow pepper, cut into 8 chunks

4 garlic cloves, unpeeled

16 cherry tomatoes, washed

Marinade

1 lime, zest and juice

1 tsp paprika

1 tbsp chopped fresh herbs

lots of freshly ground black pepper

Balsamic Drizzle

1 tbsp balsamic vinegar

1 tsp apple juice concentrate

curly endive

Pre-heat the oven to 200°C/Gas 6.

Heat the olive oil in a roasting dish, add the peppers and the unpeeled garlic cloves and roast for 20 minutes.

While the peppers are roasting, dry-fry the haloumi cubes in a large non-stick frying pan. It will ooze out a salty milky whey, which evaporates. Fry the haloumi until golden on all sides and set aside.

Marinade

Mix up the marinade. Squeeze the roasted garlic cloves out of their skins and mix the garlic purée into the marinade. Then add the roasted peppers and the haloumi. Stir well and leave to marinate for a couple of hours.

Cut 4 bamboo kebab sticks in half and soak them in water for a few minutes to prevent the sticks from burning when you grill the brochettes. Thread each stick with two cubes of haloumi, interspersed with cherry tomatoes and roasted peppers.

Grill the brochettes for a few minutes, keeping a close eye on them and turning them over several times so that they grill evenly and don't burn.

Balsamic Drizzle

By hand, mix the balsamic vinegar and apple juice concentrate together.

To serve

Serve the brochettes on a bed of curly endive and spoon on the Balsamic Drizzle with a twist of freshly ground black pepper.

Baked eggs gypsy style come from Andalusia, the beautiful southern province of Spain. They are traditionally made from whatever is in the kitchen. I have simplified this version to its vegetarian basics and spiced it up with chillies. It's delicious and very quick to make.

Andalusian Baked Eggs
Huevos a la Flamenca

SERVES 4

½ onion, very finely chopped

2 garlic cloves, crushed

1 dried red chilli, crumbled

1 knob of butter

1 tbsp olive oil

400 g tin organic chopped tomatoes

1 tsp apple juice concentrate

1 tbsp fresh basil, chopped

salt and freshly ground black pepper

4 eggs

4 tbsps single cream

Pre-heat the oven to 190°C/Gas 5.

You will need 4 × 100 ml ramekins.

Heat the butter and the olive oil in a frying pan and gently fry the onion until soft. Add the garlic and chilli and soften.

Add the tinned tomatoes and simmer for 20 minutes until the mixture has reduced to a thick chunky purée. Sweeten with the apple juice and add the fresh basil.

Warm the ramekins and divide the tomato mixture between them.

Very carefully break the eggs one at a time into a small bowl and then slip one egg into each ramekin, making sure not to break the yolks. Spoon a tablespoon of cream over each egg and sprinkle with freshly ground black pepper.

Bake in the pre-heated oven until the egg whites are set – about 20 minutes.

To serve

Eat the baked eggs at once, served with organic brown bread and butter fingers.

Tempura is the Japanese term for anything cooked in batter. The technique was introduced by the Portuguese in the 16th century. This aubergine tempura has an Indian slant as it's fried in a spicy batter and served with a yoghurt dip.

Aubergine Tempura
with a Ginger Yoghurt Dip

Sieve the gram flour, rice flour and baking powder together. Mix in the spices and salt.

Slowly mix in the lemon juice, apple juice concentrate and sunflower oil and enough water to make a smooth thick batter. Stir in the coriander and leave to stand for 30 minutes.

Heat the sunflower oil in a deep-fat fryer or wok. Dip the slices of aubergine in the batter a few at a time and pop them into the hot oil. Fry them until crisp and golden and drain on kitchen towel to absorb any excess oil.

Ginger Yoghurt Dip

In a bowl mix the soya yoghurt, soya cream, ginger juice, apple juice concentrate and chives together.

To serve

Eat the tempura at once dunked in the Ginger Yoghurt Dip.

> *To check that the oil is hot enough when deep-frying, put in a cube of bread. If it rises to the top of the oil, bubbles and quickly fries golden, the oil is hot enough. If the oil starts to smoke it is far too hot, so immediately turn off the heat and let the oil cool down.*

SERVES 4/6

300 g aubergines, sliced in slim circles

100 g gram flour
20 g rice flour
1/2 tsp baking powder
1/2 tsp ground coriander
1/2 tsp ground cumin
1/2 tsp turmeric
1/4 tsp cayenne
pinch of salt
1 tsp lemon juice
1 tsp apple juice concentrate
1 tsp sunflower oil
water to mix to a thick batter
2 tbsps fresh coriander, chopped

sunflower oil for frying

Ginger Yoghurt Dip
6 tbsps soya yoghurt
4 tbsps soya cream
1 tbsp ginger juice
1 tsp apple juice concentrate
1 tbsp fresh chives, chopped

◆ VEGAN ◆

At the restaurant we serve this vibrant coloured pâté with a delicious walnut bread baked by the local award-winning Hobbs House Bakery. It's packed with walnuts and then brushed with walnut oil for extra flavour.

Green Pea, Feta and Mint Pâté
with warm Walnut Bread

SERVES 4/6

300 g organic frozen peas

175 g feta cheese

50 g Cheddar, grated

75 g crème fraîche

1 bunch spring onions, finely sliced

1 tbsp fresh mint, chopped

juice and zest of one lemon

2 eggs

lots of freshly ground black pepper

walnut bread

Pre-heat the oven to 200°C/Gas 6.

Grease and line a 450 g loaf tin with baking parchment.

Cook the peas and drain, then refresh under cold water to retain the vibrancy of their colour.

In the food processor blend all the ingredients, except the eggs and the black pepper. Check for seasoning, before mixing in the eggs. Mix in the eggs and blend thoroughly and add black pepper to taste.

Pour the mixture into the prepared loaf tin. Cover the top with baking parchment and bake in the centre of the pre-heated oven for 40 minutes or until firm.

To serve

Serve the pâté cold, cut in slices with warm walnut bread or a nutty seeded wholewheat loaf.

Rellenos means 'stuffed' in Spanish. The idea of stuffing chillies comes from Mexico, home to an amazing range of chillies. This is a contrasting taste sensation, with the kick of the chillies soothed by the coolness of the cream cheese filling.

Wicked Cheese Chilli Rellenos
with Garlic Mayonnaise

SERVES 4

8 red chillies, fat squat ones
8 green chillies, fat squat ones
175 g full fat cream cheese
2 tbsps chives, finely chopped
salt and freshly ground black pepper

Coating

100 g plain white flour
2 eggs, beaten
115 g breadcrumbs

sunflower oil for deep-frying

Garlic Mayonnaise

65 ml soya milk
1/2 tbsp cider vinegar
1/2 tbsp lemon juice
2 garlic cloves, crushed
1 tsp whole grain mustard
150 ml sunflower oil
salt and freshly ground black pepper

First blanch the chillies. Heat a large saucepan of water and when the water comes to the boil plunge in the whole chillies and simmer for one minute. Remove them with a slotted spoon and leave to cool. The idea is to just soften the skins.

Cut a small slit below the stem of each chilli pepper and remove all the seeds and pith.

Mix the chives into the cream cheese and season with black pepper and salt if needed. Carefully stuff each chilli with the cream cheese mixture, taking care not to break it open too much. Don't worry if the cream cheese is stuck to the outside of the chillies as they will be covered with batter.

Coating

Beat the eggs into the flour to make a thin batter. Dunk each chilli into the egg batter and then coat with breadcrumbs. Freeze the stuffed chillies for 15 minutes to firm them up, then deep-fry until golden.

Garlic Mayonnaise

Place all the ingredients except the oil, salt and pepper into the food processor. Blend until well mixed.

In exactly the same way as making classic mayonnaise, pour the oil in very slowly whilst the food processor is running. The consistency of the mixture will gradually thicken as the oil is trickled in.

Finally, add sea salt and freshly ground black pepper to taste.

To serve

Eat the Rellenos at once, dipped in the Garlic Mayonnaise.

Tempeh Goreng is one of the most popular Javanese fried snacks and is always served with Sambal Kecap and a handful of aromatic herbs.

Tempeh Goreng
with Sambal Kecap

SERVES 4

150 g tempeh

Marinade

2 tbsps tamari

2 tbsps boiling water

1 clove garlic, peeled and crushed

1 tsp ginger juice

1/2 tsp kecap manis or brown sugar

1/4 tsp hot chilli sauce

sunflower oil for shallow-frying

aromatic herbs; sprigs of fresh mint, watercress and basil

Sambal Kecap

1 red chilli, deseeded and thinly sliced

1 shallot, peeled and thinly sliced

2 tbsps tamari

1 tsp kecap manis or brown sugar

1 tbsp water

1 tsp lime juice

Slice the tempeh into slim 2.5 cm long fingers and put into a bowl.

Marinade

Make up the marinade by mixing all the ingredients in a bowl. Pour this over the tempeh and marinate for 30 minutes, stirring occasionally to ensure that it's evenly covered. The tempeh should absorb most of the marinade.

Drain off any remaining marinade, pat the tempeh dry with kitchen paper and shallow-fry in sunflower oil until golden and crisp. Drain on kitchen paper.

Sambal Kecap

Place the chopped chillis and shallots in a small bowl. Mix together the tamari, kecap manis, water and lime juice and add this mixture to the chillis and shallots. Leave to marinate for 30 minutes.

To serve

Serve at once with Sambal Kecap and a handful of aromatic herbs.

Tempeh comes from Indonesia and is made of compressed, lightly fermented soya beans. Packed full of protein, it is free from cholesterol and has a delicious nutty flavour and chewy texture.

Kecap manis is a sweet dark soy sauce.

◆ **VEGAN** ◆

A variation on Scotch eggs with a mashed potato outer and a blue cheese and pear filling. As they are very rich, one is scrumptious, two are delicious and three are too many!

Pear and Blue Cheese Truffles

Boil the sweet potato and ordinary potato separately as they cook at different times. Drain them and mash the potatoes together with the butter, Tabasco, basil, salt and freshly ground black pepper.

Mix the pear and blue cheese together with your fingers into 18 tight little balls.

With the potato mixture make 18 ping-pong sized balls; press your thumb into each potato ball to make a cavity large enough to fit in a pear and blue cheese ball. With your fingers, push a pear and blue cheese ball into a potato ball and close the cavity.

Roll each ball in beaten egg, coat with crushed nuts and shallow-fry until golden.

To serve

Heat the redcurrant jelly with the lemon juice and drizzle over the truffles.

Make sure that the sweet potato is the variety with pink flesh, rather than white. The pink fleshed variety is sweet and is easy to mash, the white is much more fibrous, tends to turn grey when cooked and is more akin to cassava in taste.

SERVES 4/6

225 g sweet potato, peeled and cubed

225 g potato, peeled and chopped

25 g butter

1/2 tsp Tabasco

1 tbsp fresh basil, chopped

salt and freshly ground black pepper

1/2 pear (75 g), peeled, cored and finely diced

115 g blue cheese, cut into small cubes

1 egg, beaten

75 g hazelnuts, whizzed

75 g cashews, whizzed

sunflower oil for shallow-frying

4 tbsps redcurrant jelly

1 tbsp lemon juice

Wander through the food stalls in a Bangkok market at dusk and you'll see steam rising from bubbling woks and hear constant chatter as people grab a snack on their way home. It's a joy to watch rice cakes being deep-fried, drizzled with sauce and handed to you to eat at once.

Tiny Thai Rice Cakes
with Sweet Chilli Sauce

Cook the two types of rice separately as they require different cooking times and methods. Cook the wild rice in plenty of water, for about 45 minutes. You can tell when it's cooked as the grains pop out of their cases. It's crucial that wild rice is cooked thoroughly, if undercooked it will explode when fried. Drain and set aside.

Cook the Thai rice in enough water to cover the rice by 1 cm. Cover the pan, bring to the boil and simmer for only a couple of minutes. Take the pan off the heat and leave covered for 10 minutes, in which time the rice will absorb all the water. Fluff up the rice with a fork and set aside.

Cook the sweet potato and ordinary potato separately as they take different times to cook. Drain very well and mash.

Make sure the rice and the potatoes are well drained before mixing them together; a sloppy mix is difficult to fry. Mix the cooked rice and mashed potatoes together.

Finely chop the garlic, red chilli and ginger, or if you have a labour saving mini processor, just whiz the garlic, chilli and ginger together. Mix the sliced spring onion with the coriander.

Combine all the ingredients with your hands, making a mixture with a consistency that will form into soft balls. Taste for seasoning.

Shape the mixture into balls about half the size of a ping-pong ball. Roll in rice flour and gently flatten into 4 cm round patties. The mix will make about 18 rice cakes. Shallow-fry in sunflower oil ½ cm deep until golden on both sides.

To serve

Eat the Rice Cakes at once, dipped in sweet chilli sauce.

SERVES 4/6

25 g wild rice

75 g Thai fragrant white rice

100 g sweet potato, peeled

100 g potato, peeled

large pinch of salt

4 garlic cloves, peeled

1 red chilli, sliced

2 cm piece of root ginger, peeled and chopped

2 spring onions, finely sliced

2 tbsps fresh coriander, chopped

100 g rice flour for rolling

sunflower oil for frying

Sweet chilli sauce is available in small bottles from supermarkets, but if you get addicted to it, large absurdly good value bottles are available from Asian stores.

♦ VEGAN ♦

These triangular filo parcels, filled with fresh spinach, salty feta and crunchy aromatic pink peppercorns, are easy to make. Best eaten piping hot straight from the oven.

Spinach and Feta Filo Parcels

SERVES 4/6

16 sheets of filo measuring approx 25 cms x 18 cms

25 g butter, melted

250 g fresh spinach, destalked and washed

100 g feta cheese, crumbled

2 garlic cloves, crushed

2 spring onions, finely chopped

1 tbsp pink peppercorns

1/2 tsp cayenne

salt and freshly ground black pepper

Buy filo pastry, fresh or frozen, from supermarkets. Defrost for an hour before using. Any leftover filo pastry can be put back in the freezer. Just make sure that it's well wrapped in clingfilm, otherwise it will dry out..

Pink peppercorns are not actually peppercorns but the aromatic dried red berries of a tree, Schinus Molle. They have a brittle outer shell enclosing a small pepper-like seed.

Pre-heat the oven to 200°C/Gas 6.

Steam the spinach, drain and squeeze out all the liquid. Then chop roughly and set aside.

Crush the pink peppercorns with a pestle and mortar.

In a large bowl mix the garlic, spring onions, pink peppercorns and cayenne together. Mix in the feta cheese and chopped spinach and add salt and freshly ground black pepper.

To make into parcels take one sheet of filo and, with the short side facing you, brush with melted butter. Fold the two long sides towards the middle, making a strip 6cm wide and brush with butter. Place a dessertspoon size portion of filling at the bottom left corner of the strip. Pick up the corner with the filling and fold this over so that the bottom edge meets the side edge and forms a right angle triangle. Continue folding over from side to side into neat triangles until you reach the end of the strip. Brush the finished triangle with butter and place on a greased baking sheet.

Continue making parcels in this manner, placing them on the baking sheet so that they don't touch, as they will puff up during baking. Aim to make 16 parcels.

Bake in the pre-heated oven for 15 minutes until golden.

To serve

Serve hot, straight from the oven.

This dish is best made in the summer with young leeks and small firm courgettes. You will need to marinate them for at least 24 hours to allow the flavours to infuse into the vegetables.

Green Vegetables
in a Wine and Apple Marinade, served with Toasted Ciabatta

Pre-heat the oven to 220°C/Gas 7.

Prepare the vegetables, washing the leeks really well to remove any grit.

In a baking dish mix all the vegetables together, drizzle with the olive oil and roast in the pre-heated oven until tender. This should take about 20 minutes but it does depend on the size you have cut the vegetables. Stir in the green olives and roast for a further 5 minutes.

Wine and Apple Marinade

While the vegetables are roasting, make the marinade by simply mixing the ingredients together.

Put the hot roasted vegetables into a serving bowl and pour over the marinade. Mix well and leave to marinate in the fridge for at least 24 hours. Take out of the fridge an hour before serving.

To serve

Decorate the vegtables with fresh dill and a twist of black pepper and serve with toasted ciabatta to mop up the juices.

This white wine and apple juice marinade is delicious with a myriad of vegetables. Try it with asparagus, artichoke hearts and baby broad beans.

SERVES 4/6

100 g shallots, sliced

100 g leeks, cut into 2 cm thick rounds

100 g courgettes, cut into thick matchsticks

100 g green pepper, cut into matchsticks

4 tbsps olive oil

100 g green pitted olives

Wine and Apple Marinade

150 ml white wine

2 tbsps apple juice concentrate

50 ml apple juice

50 ml water

1 tbsp tamari

1 tbsp fresh dill, chopped

fresh dill for decoration

freshly ground black pepper

ciabatta loaf

♦ VEGAN ♦

Deep fried Momo are a traditional Tibetan dish, rather like miniature pasties. They are eaten scalding hot, dunked into Shamdur sauce and washed down with Yak butter tea. Very warming at an altitude of 5000 metres.

Tibetan Momo
with Shamdur Sauce

SERVES 8

Pastry

200 g plain white flour

200 g wholemeal flour

1 tsp bicarbonate of soda

water to mix to a soft dough

285 g plain tofu in small cubes

Marinade

4 tbsps shoyu

1 tbsp sweet chilli sauce

1 tsp apple juice concentrate

2 cm fresh ginger root, grated

1 tbsp sunflower oil

1 bunch spring onions, finely chopped

1 green chilli, finely chopped

4 garlic cloves, finely chopped

½ tsp ground cumin

½ tsp ground nutmeg

½ tsp ground cinnamon

100 g shiitake mushrooms, finely chopped

Salt and freshly ground black pepper

Sunflower oil for deep-frying

Pastry

First make the pastry. Mix the flours together, then add the bicarbonate of soda, making sure there are no lumps. Mix well and then slowly add cold water, a little at a time. Use your hands to form into a soft dough and set aside.

Drain the liquid from the tofu and cut into little cubes.

Marinade

For the marinade, mix together the shoyu, chilli sauce and apple juice concentrate and add the squeezed juice from the grated ginger. Add the tofu and leave to marinate for 30 minutes.

Lightly stir-fry the spring onion, chilli and garlic in the sunflower oil. Add the spices and the mushrooms and stir-fry for a couple of minutes. Add the tofu and all the marinade and stir-fry for a few more minutes until the mixture has absorbed most of the liquid. Season to taste.

On a well-floured surface, roll out the pastry to ¼ cm thickness and cut out about 20 x 18 cm circles. Take a large teaspoon of the filling and place it in the middle of each pastry circle. Fold the circle in half making a half moon shape. Pinch the edges together firmly so that none of the juices can escape when cooking. The idea is to get the Momo to sit up, so that the pinched edge will be uppermost. Squash the Momo down onto its base so that it looks like a mini pasty. Pinch the top edge to look like a three-cornered hat.

Heat the oil for deep-frying and fry until golden. Alternatively, bake until crisp.

◆ **VEGAN** ◆

Shamdur Sauce

Mix the crushed garlic, shoyu, sweet chilli sauce and tomato purée together to make up the Shamdur sauce.

To serve

Eat the Momos piping hot and dipped into the Shamdur sauce.

Shamdur Sauce

2 garlic cloves, crushed

2 tbsps shoyu

1 tbsp sweet chilli sauce

1 tsp tomato purée

◆ VEGAN ◆

Soups

Traditionally soups were a meal in themselves and more akin to a stew. The name is derived from the old English 'sop' and was a term applied to hard bread dipped in broth. When people became more affluent and could afford to eat more than one course, soup became a part of a meal rather than one in itself.

Every country has its speciality. In Thailand it's tom yam, in India it's rasams. It's miso soup in Japan and potajes in Spain, whilst in Italy it's minestrone. It's hariras in North Africa, bouillabaisse in France and chowder in the USA.

Not only are they regional but they are also seasonal. In winter they are packed with root vegetables, beans and lentils; and in summer they become light, vibrant, smooth and are often served cold.

Soups are incredibly quick and easy to make and far more satisfying than buying expensive so-called 'fresh soups'. The only time-consuming part is making a stock, which I recommend making in bulk and freezing in small portions. However, when I'm short of time I use a vegetable bouillon powder instead.

The soups I have chosen here are just a taster, as with other recipes, you should experiment with different ingredients yourself.

Why does beetroot soup have such bad press? Is it its association with Russian cooking or cabbage? I find it delicious and the colour fantastic. At the restaurant those that have this soup always exclaim how they enjoyed it. The difficulty is in persuading people to choose it.

Bortsch

SERVES 4/6

500 g raw beetroot

1 onion, chopped

2 tbsps olive oil

2 garlic cloves, chopped

3 tomatoes, cored and chopped

2 tsps vegetable bouillon powder

750 ml water

1 orange, zest and juice

salt and freshly ground black pepper

1 tsp tamari

sour cream or soya cream

chives, chopped, for decoration

Wash the earth off the beetroot, cut the leaves off at about 10 cm leaving the roots on. Boil them whole and unpeeled until cooked, approx 1 hour. Leave to cool.

Fry the onion in the olive oil until translucent, add the garlic and fry for a couple more minutes.

Peel the beetroot, under water to avoid staining your hands purple, and chop it up on a non-staining surface.

Add the chopped beetroot and tomatoes to the onions, together with the bouillon and the zest of the orange. Add 750 ml of water, bring to the boil and simmer gently for 15 minutes.

Purée the soup in a food processor or a liquidiser and add the orange juice. You may need to add a little more water to achieve a smooth, soupy consistency. Season with salt, a dash of tamari and lots of freshly ground black pepper.

To serve

To serve, swirl with sour cream or soya cream and sprinkle with chopped chives.

The best time to buy beetroot is in late summer. Choose small ones with the leaves still attached and looking fresh. Always cook beetroot whole and unpeeled, because if you cut beetroot it bleeds into the cooking water and looses its colour. The leaves are edible, but rather bitter.

◆ **VEGAN** ◆

This is one of our head chef, Charlotte's, chunky vegetable soups enriched with a peppery rocket pistou.

Summer Vegetable Soup
with Rocket Pistou

SERVES 4

1 small onion, chopped

1 tbsp olive oil

2 garlic cloves, chopped

1 medium leek, sliced

1 bulb fennel, finely sliced

1 medium carrot, finely cubed

1 medium courgette, cubed

1 litre vegetable stock, made with 1 tbsp vegetable bouillon powder

1/2 lemon, juiced

salt and freshly ground black pepper

Rocket Pistou

2 garlic cloves

25 ml extra virgin olive oil

1 tsp apple juice concentrate

50 g rocket

2 tbsps vegetarian Parmesan, grated

Fry the onion in the olive oil until soft, add the garlic and stir-fry for a minute.

Add the leek, fennel and carrot and fry for 5 minutes. Then add the courgette and fry for another couple of minutes.

Pour in the stock, bring to the boil and simmer until the vegetables are only just cooked and still have a bite to them. Squeeze in the lemon juice and season to taste.

Rocket Pistou

In a food processor whiz the garlic, olive oil and apple juice concentrate. Add the rocket and whiz to a smooth consistency.

Stir in the vegetarian Parmesan.

To serve

Serve the soup hot, topped with a swirl of Rocket Pistou.

Rocket has a curly green leaf about the size of a dandelion leaf and is best when young and tender. It is very easy to grow from seed in the garden or in tubs.

Gazpacho, which originates from Andalusia, is traditionally eaten by workers for a cool refreshing lunch. It is always eaten raw and must be ice cold. Ripe sweet tomatoes are crucial to making a rich flavoursome soup, so gazpacho is best made in late summer.

Gazpacho
Cold Southern Spanish Soup

Choose ripe flavoursome tomatoes for this soup. Slice the skins and cover with boiling water. Leave to stand for a few minutes and then peel off the skins with a small knife. Cut the peeled tomatoes in half, remove the cores and seeds and chop the flesh.

With a vegetable peeler, peel strips off the cucumber, so that some of the skin is left on. Slice it lengthways and take out the seeds, then chop, retaining a few diced cubes for the garnish.

Dice the red pepper, retaining a few diced cubes for the garnish.

Chop the onion and garlic and mix all the vegetables together.

Soak the white bread in water, squeeze out and mix with the vegetables. Add the olive oil, vinegar, tomato purée, salt and cayenne.

In a blender or food processor blend the gazpacho. It is easier to blend in a couple of batches, using the water to make a smooth soup each time. Check for seasoning and refrigerate for a couple of hours.

To serve

Serve the soup ice cold with little bowls of cucumber, red pepper and crouton garnish on the side.

SERVES 4/6

10 ripe tomatoes

1 cucumber

1 red pepper

1/2 small red onion

2 garlic cloves

2 slices white bread, crusts removed

3 tbsps olive oil

2 tbsps red wine vinegar

1 tsp tomato purée

1 tsp coarse sea salt

pinch of cayenne

300 ml cold water

Garnishes

small croutons, fried in olive oil

cucumber, diced small

red pepper, diced small

To make croutons, remove the crusts from slices of bread and cut the bread into small cubes, about 1 cm in diameter. In a small frying pan heat enough olive oil to shallow-fry the croutons. When the oil is hot, gently put in the croutons and fry until golden on all sides. Take out with a slotted spoon and drain on kitchen towel to remove any excess oil. I do prefer white bread for croutons as the finish is much crisper.

♦ VEGAN ♦

In France, I have always been intrigued by bowls of 'bouillabaisse', fish soup, dunked with French bread spread with spicy rouille. This is our vegetarian version. The essential flavouring of saffron gives the soup an aromatic quality and adds a soft golden colour.

Roasted Garlic Soup
with Rouille and French Bread

Pre-heat the oven to 200°C/Gas 6.

Wrap the whole garlic bulbs in silver foil, place in the oven and roast until soft and squishy – about 15 minutes. Meanwhile heat the olive oil in a heavy-bottomed saucepan and fry the onions until they are translucent.

Add the potato, tomatoes, boiling water, saffron and herbs and boil furiously for 10 to 15 minutes so that the olive oil and water amalgamate.

Remove the garlic from the oven and leave to cool until you can handle it. Squeeze the garlic cloves out of their skins into a bowl, mix with some broth from the soup and purée until smooth. Stir the puréed garlic into the soup and simmer for a few minutes. Season to taste with salt and black pepper.

Rouille

Remove the crusts from the bread and soak in water for a couple of minutes, then squeeze out all the water. Cut the pepper in half and roast it in a hot oven or under the grill until charred, leave to cool and then peel off the skin, discard the seeds and chop.

In a food processor, blend the soaked bread, red pepper, garlic, tomato purée and olive oil into a very smooth purée. Season to taste with cayenne and salt.

To serve

There are two different ways to serve rouille, each equally correct: either spread the rouille on the crisped French bread, place in the bottom of the soup bowl and ladle the soup over, or just eat the bread and rouille with the soup. Sprinkle the soup with Gruyère for the authentic stringy touch.

SERVES 4

2 bulbs of garlic, whole

2 large onions, finely sliced

50 ml olive oil

1 potato, peeled and sliced into half moons

4 tomatoes, cored and diced

750 ml boiling water

pinch of saffron

1 bay leaf

1 tsp fresh thyme, chopped

1 tbsp fresh parsley, chopped

salt and lots of freshly ground black pepper

Rouille

4 slices white bread

4 garlic cloves, chopped

1 red pepper

1 tsp tomato purée

4 tbsps olive oil

pinch cayenne pepper

salt

French bread, sliced and crisped in the oven.

grated Gruyère

This health-restoring Japanese-style soup is very nutritious, light and colourful. Best eaten at once, as it quickly loses its vibrancy. If you are in a hurry, use one teaspoon of vegetable bouillon powder instead of making the stock.

Miso Ramen Soup
with Tofu and Seaweed

SERVES 4

Stock

1.5 litres water

1 medium onion, quartered

2 carrots, cut in half

2 celery stalks, cut in half

1/4 of a fennel bulb

2 bay leaves

4 parsley stems

8 whole black peppercorns

Miso Ramen Soup

2 tbsps arame seaweed

100 g soba ramen noodles

750 ml stock

4 tbsps shoyu

1 tbsp ginger juice

1 carrot, peeled, halved and cut in thin half moons

100 g mangetout peas, cut in half

4 spring onions, in rings

100 g plain tofu, in small cubes

2 tbsps miso

handful of coriander leaves for garnish

Stock

Put all the ingredients in a large saucepan, bring to the boil, turn down the heat and simmer gently until the vegetables are cooked and the stock has reduced by a quarter – about one hour. Strain the stock, keeping the liquid and discarding the vegetables.

Miso Ramen Soup

Soak the seaweed in boiling water for 15 minutes.

Boil the soba ramen noodles in plenty of water for 6 minutes, drain and divide between 4 bowls.

Bring the stock to the boil and add the seaweed plus the soaking water and the shoyu, ginger juice and sliced carrots and boil for 5 minutes.

Then add the mangetout peas, spring onions, tofu and miso and simmer gently for a couple of minutes.

To serve

Pour the miso soup over the soba ramen noodles, garnish with coriander and eat at once.

Japanese soba ramen noodles are made from buckwheat flour.

Arame is seaweed shredded into very small strands and has a mild salty flavour.

Miso is made by fermenting soya beans, rice barley or wheat with salt. Miso is very nutritious, rich in protein, minerals, B vitamins and calcium. It is a living food containing enzymes from the fermentation process and is always added at the end of cooking to avoid killing these healthy enzymes.

♦ VEGAN ♦

*This is an autumnal soup, with the warming quality of ginger,
the sweetness of parsnips and a wonderful ochre
colour from the squash.*

Onion Squash, Parsnip and Ginger Soup

Fry the onion in the olive oil until soft and translucent. Add the garlic and ginger and stir-fry until fragrant.

Add the onion squash, parsnips and vegetable stock. Bring to the boil, turn down and simmer gently until the squash and parsnips are cooked.

Purée the soup in a food processor or liquidiser, adding more water if it's too thick.

To serve

Add the lemon juice, season well and decorate with chopped coriander.

SERVES 4

2 tbsps olive oil

1 small onion, chopped

2 garlic cloves, chopped

6 cm piece of ginger, peeled and finely chopped

500 g onion squash, peeled and roughly chopped

250 g parsnips, peeled and roughly chopped

1 litre vegetable stock, made with 1 tbsp vegetable bouillon powder

1 tbsp lemon juice

salt and freshly ground black pepper

fresh coriander, chopped for decoration

Onion squash is a winter squash that is ready to harvest in October and can be stored throughout the winter. It is shaped just like a giant onion, with bright orange skin and flesh to match. If you can't find onion squash use butternut squash instead.

♦ VEGAN ♦

QUICK MEALS

Bruschetta, Wraps etc.

Bruschetta were, traditionally, Tuscan snacks made to allow people to taste the new olive oil harvest. They are thick slices of Italian country style sourdough bread, toasted, rubbed with garlic and drizzled with fruity extra virgin olive oil. They taste even better with just a sprinkling of Maldon salt.

Wraps are my favourite substitute for a sandwich, because they have less bread, more filling and are so simple to make. All you need is a pack of wheat tortillas and your choice of salad ingredients. They are one of the most popular lunchtime dishes that we serve in the restaurant.

Bagels are Jewish bread rolls formed into a ring and lightly boiled before baking. The name comes from the German word 'beugel', meaning a ring or bracelet. They make a quick and versatile snack when sliced in half, spread with homemade pesto, topped with tomatoes, red onions and chunks of goats' cheese and slid under the grill to melt and brown.

Ciabatta means 'slipper' in Italian, and with a bit of imagination can appear shaped rather like one. Their texture is full of holes from being made with a wet dough and they have a mildly soured flavour which is enriched by olive oil.

I ate my first wrap in Melbourne, Australia and thought it was a fantastic alternative to a sandwich. The filling for this one is light, flavoursome and summery.

Sunny Sensation Wrap
with Yoghurt and Mustard Dressing

SERVES 4

4 wheat tortillas

250 g haloumi, thinly sliced

romano or cos lettuce, shredded

1 avocado, peeled and sliced

8 tomatoes, quartered

1 red pepper, thinly sliced

handful of alfalfa sprouts

8 spring onions, sliced

Yoghurt and Mustard Dressing

125 g plain yoghurt

2 tbsps double cream

1 tbsp Dijon mustard

1 tsp apple juice concentrate

Dry-fry the haloumi in a frying pan until golden on both sides. Prepare all the salad vegetables.

Yoghurt and Mustard Dressing

Make the Yoghurt and Mustard Dressing by simply mixing all the ingredients together in a bowl.

Warm the tortillas under the grill or in a dry frying pan. Spread each tortilla sparingly with Yoghurt and Mustard Dressing, cover with shredded lettuce and top with the avocado, tomatoes, red pepper, alfalfa sprouts and spring onions. Cover with the hot grilled haloumi slices and spoon on the Yoghurt and Mustard Dressing.

Roll up, cut in half and eat at once.

A tortilla is a thin pancake made from maize flour or wheat flour, shaped and flattened by hand and cooked on both sides on a griddle until dry. They can be filled, wrapped or rolled as tacos, wraps or enchiladas. Not to be confused with Spanish tortillas, which are omelettes.

These Bruschetta are quick, easy to make, and gorgeous when drizzled with an extra virgin olive oil.

Aubergine, Courgette and Cherry Tomato Bruschetta ◆VEGAN◆

SERVES 6

½ aubergine, diced small

4 tbsps extra virgin olive oil

2 courgettes, diced

125 g cherry tomatoes, halved

1 tbsp lemon juice

lots of fresh basil, chopped

salt and freshly ground black pepper

Pre-heat the oven to 225°C/Gas 7.

Roast the aubergine in the olive oil for 10 minutes in the pre-heated oven, then add the courgettes and roast until the courgettes are just cooked. Decant into a large bowl and add the halved cherry tomatoes, lemon juice and basil and season with salt and freshly ground black pepper.

Flageolet and Artichoke Bruschetta

SERVES 6

425 g tin flageolet beans, sugar free, drained and rinsed

400 g tin artichoke hearts, drained

2 garlic cloves, crushed

50 g vegetarian Parmesan, grated

4 tbsps extra virgin olive oil

1 tbsp lemon juice

handful of freshly chopped parsley

sea salt and freshly ground black pepper

To make the flageolet and artichoke topping you'll need a food processor. Place the flageolet beans, artichoke hearts, garlic, Parmesan, olive oil, lemon juice and parsley in the food processor and whiz to a chunky consistency.

Season to taste with salt and freshly ground black pepper.

Making up the bruschetta

Toast 6 slices of country style white bread, Pugliese is traditional, on both sides. Rub the hot toast with a cut garlic clove and drizzle with extra virgin olive oil. Spread the bruschetta with your choice of topping and serve at once.

This is a variation on a Welsh rarebit, but with an Italian theme, using sun-dried tomatoes and mushrooms instead of cheese. Serve as a topping for ciabatta with a salad, for a light lunch.

Sun-dried Tomato and Creamy Mushroom Ciabatta

Cut the sun-dried tomatoes into small pieces with a pair of kitchen scissors and soak in boiling water for 1/2 hour until the tomatoes have rehydrated. Strain off the water and retain for stock.

In a saucepan sauté the garlic and thinly sliced mushrooms in butter for a few minutes. Mix the cornflour with a little cold milk to a smooth paste and add to the sautéed mushrooms. Add half the milk and bring to the boil, stirring all the time. When the mushroom sauce begins to thicken add the remaining milk and keep on stirring until the sauce has thickened. Then add the drained sun-dried tomatoes, bouillon powder and shoyu, simmer for a few minutes, stirring well. Finally, add the cream and season to taste.

To serve, cut the ciabatta bread lengthways into portion sized pieces, spread the cut side with the sun-dried tomato mixture and place under the grill until the topping bubbles.

Garnish with parsley and serve at once with a light green salad.

SERVES 6

1 ciabatta bread

50 g sun-dried tomatoes, not in oil

200 g mushrooms, thinly sliced

2 garlic cloves, finely chopped

30 g butter

250 ml milk

1 level tbsp cornflour

1 tsp vegetable bouillon powder

1 tbsp shoyu

65 ml double cream

salt and freshly ground black pepper, to taste

parsley, chopped, for decoration

Ciabatta literally means 'slipper' in Italian, and with a bit of imagination, the bread is shaped rather like a slipper. It has a holey texture, a mildly soured flavour and is enriched with olive oil.

Lavash bread is a very thin and crispy ancient Arab bread, that is traditionally baked in a wood burning tandoor oven. You can buy lavash bread in Middle Eastern stores and some supermarkets, but if you can't find any, use wheat tortillas instead.

Lebanese Wrap

SERVES 4

4 Lebanese lavash bread or wheat tortillas

4 tbsps olive oil

1 leek, sliced in 1cm chunks

1 medium courgette, cut in 1cm chunks

1 bulb fennel, thinly sliced

100 g green olives, pitted

freshly ground black pepper

pesto, to spread on the lavash bread

iceberg lettuce, shredded

200 g labna balls or feta, cut into cubes

handful fresh mint, chopped

extra virgin olive oil, to drizzle

Basil Pesto

75 g pinenuts, toasted

75 g hazelnuts, roasted, and skins rubbed off

3 garlic cloves, peeled

75 g fresh basil

175 ml olive oil

2 tbsps lemon juice

1 tbsp white wine vinegar

1 tbsp apple juice concentrate

salt and freshly ground black pepper

Pre-heat the oven to 225°C/Gas 7.

Heat the olive oil in a roasting tin in the pre-heated oven. Add the leek, courgette and fennel, stir well and roast for 20 minutes. Add the green olives and lots of black pepper and roast for another 10 minutes.

Basil Pesto

In a food processor or pestle and mortar, grind the pinenuts and hazelnuts roughly and then decant them into a bowl and set aside.

Purée the garlic in a little of the olive oil, then add the basil and the rest of the olive oil and purée just enough to break up the basil. Add the lemon juice, apple juice concentrate and vinegar and blend quickly. Pour the basil and garlic mixture into the ground nuts and stir in.

Spread each lavash bread with pesto and cover with a layer of iceberg lettuce. Top this off with the roasted vegetables and olives, add the labna balls or feta cubes and sprinkle with mint.

Finally, drizzle with extra virgin olive oil, roll up, cut in half and eat.

Labna is a creamy yoghurt goats' cheese. In Lebanon they roll the labna into little balls, dip them in olive oil and coat them with chopped fresh herbs.

Quern bread is an old-fashioned solid loaf flavoured with molasses, made by our bakers, Hobbs House, in Chipping Sodbury. If you can't find it a dense, dark, thinly sliced rye bread is a good alternative.

Black Olive and Caper Tapénade
with Toasted Quern Bread

SERVES 12

100 g black olives, pitted

60g capers, drained and rinsed

1 garlic clove, finely chopped

½ small red onion, finely chopped

2 tbsps olive oil

2 tbsps lemon juice

1 tbsp apple juice concentrate

lots of freshly ground black pepper

quern bread, thinly sliced

Put the olives, capers, garlic and onion in a food processor. Blend to a chunky consistency. Add all the remaining ingredients and blend again.

The consistency should be spreadable with little chunks of olive and caper remaining. Check for seasoning.

Very lightly toast the quern bread and spread with the tapénade. Any leftover tapénade will keep in the fridge for a week or two.

The name bagel comes from the German word 'beugel', meaning ring, which describes the shape of the bread. They are cooked in a unique way by being boiled in water for a few seconds before baking, giving them their characteristic chewy crust.

Goats' Cheese and Pesto Bagel
with Walnuts and Balsamic Vinaigrette

Cut the bagels in half, spread with pesto, top with sliced red onion, tomatoes cut in eighths and the goats' cheese. Sprinkle with walnuts.

Rocket Pesto

In a food processor or pestle and mortar grind the pinenuts and walnuts roughly and then decant them into a bowl and set aside.

Purée the garlic in a little of the olive oil, then add the rocket and the rest of the olive oil and purée just enough to break up the rocket. Add the lemon juice, apple juice concentrate and vinegar and blend quickly. Pour the rocket and garlic mixture into the ground nuts and stir in.

Place under a hot grill and grill until the goats' cheese begins to brown. Serve with salad leaves and a drizzle of balsamic vinaigrette.

SERVES 2

2 plain organic bagels

2 tbsps pesto

2 tomatoes, cut into eighths

1 small red onion, thinly sliced

100 g goats' cheese, sliced

50 g walnuts

balsamic vinaigrette

salad leaves

Rocket Pesto

75 g pinenuts, toasted

75 g walnuts, toasted

3 garlic cloves, peeled

75 g fresh rocket

175 ml olive oil

2 tbsps lemon juice

1 tbsp white wine vinegar

1 tbsp apple juice concentrate

salt and freshly ground black pepper

Capricorn goats' cheese is my favourite for grilling.
Organic bagels are available from wholefood shops and some supermarkets.

Pasta

Popular legend has it that Marco Polo introduced noodles to Italy on his return overland from China. Although the origins of pasta are still being argued over, the importance of pasta is strongest in southern Italy, suggesting Greek or Arab origins.

It is now the most central food in Italian cooking, with every region having its own recipes. It's made with a hard durum Italian wheat flour, which has a high protein level.

There are hundreds of different shapes and sizes of pasta. The shape decrees the type of sauce it will be served with. Tubular pasta, such as penne, is best with creamy thick sauces. Long thin pasta such as linguine and tagliatelle are best with oily herby sauces.

The key to good pasta is to serve it 'al dente', while it still has bite to it. You will get better results from a good quality dried pasta than from supermarket fresh pasta, which is very easy to overcook.

The cooking method is the same whichever you use. To a large saucepan of salted boiling water add a tablespoon of olive oil to stop the pasta sticking together. Bring it back to the boil and add the pasta. Fresh takes about 3–5 minutes and dried 10–12 minutes. Once cooked, drain the pasta and serve immediately.

This is a rich creamy pasta with a subtle mushroom flavour enlivened with the anise flavour of the tarragon.

Oyster Mushroom and Courgette Tagliatelle
with Fresh Tarragon

SERVES 4

1 medium onion, sliced

1 tbsp olive oil

4 garlic cloves, finely chopped

125 g oyster mushrooms, shredded

125 g chestnut mushrooms, quartered

2 small courgettes, cut in half moons

100 ml dry white wine

1 tbsp shoyu

125 g single cream

salt and lots of freshly ground black pepper

small handful fresh tarragon, chopped

75 g – 100 g tagliatelle per serving

Fry the onion in the olive oil until golden. Add the garlic and stir-fry for a couple of minutes. Add the mushrooms and courgettes and stir-fry for a couple more minutes.

Pour in the wine and shoyu and simmer until the courgettes are just cooked. Then stir in the cream, season to taste and add as much tarragon as you like.

Cook the tagliatelle following the instructions in cooking techniques on page 201.

In a large saucepan heat the sauce and stir in the cooked tagliatelle a little at a time, until the proportions of pasta to sauce look right.

To serve

Serve at once with a green leaf salad.

Shoyu is a naturally fermented soya sauce made from soya beans, wheat, salt and water.

Rich, earthy and dark, this one is for autumnal nights. The sauce is a combination of strong flavours which come from the caramelised onions, roasted garlic, mushrooms, rosemary and walnuts.

Rosemary Linguine
with Onion, Roasted Garlic, Mushroom and Walnut Sauce

SERVES 4

2 tbsps extra virgin olive oil

1 sprig fresh rosemary, destemmed

1 tbsp fresh thyme, destemmed

1 bay leaf

2 red onions, peeled and thinly sliced

250 g mushrooms, quartered

1 whole bulb of garlic, unpeeled

125 g walnuts, toasted

125 ml red wine

125 ml water

1 tbsp shoyu

salt and freshly ground black pepper

75 g – 100 g fresh linguine pasta per serving

freshly chopped parsley

Heat the olive oil in a frying pan, add the fresh herbs and stir-fry until fragrant.

Add the onions and sauté until soft, brown and caramelised. Add the mushrooms and stir-fry until they begin to brown at the edges.

In a hot oven, roast the unpeeled garlic until soft, this shoud take about 15 minutes. Leave to cool and then squeeze the garlic cloves out of their skins.

Toast the walnuts lightly under the grill.

Add the roasted garlic, toasted walnuts, wine, water and shoyu to the mushroom and onion mixture. Bring to the boil, turn down the heat and simmer until the sauce is reduced to a syrupy consistency. Season to taste with salt and freshly ground black pepper.

Cook the linguine according to the instructions in cooking techniques on page 201.

Heat the sauce in a large pan and then add the cooked linguine, a little at a time, until the proportions of pasta to sauce look right. You may not need all the linguine. Mix the linguine in and serve at once.

To serve

Sprinkle with parsley and serve with a simple crisp, green salad, made with little gem lettuce.

◆ VEGAN ◆

A rich, vibrantly colourful pasta dish combining the saltiness of haloumi with the sweetness of roasted red peppers.

Penne with Spinach, Rocket and Haloumi

Wash the red peppers, slice them in half and take out the seeds. Then place them under a hot grill until the skins are blackened. For ease of peeling put the roasted peppers into a bowl, seal the top of the bowl with clingfilm and leave for 20 minutes. When you take them out the skins should peel off easily. Cut the pepper into thin slices and set aside.

To dry-fry the haloumi, cut into small cubes and place in a non-stick frying pan over a moderate heat and fry, turning once, until golden. This will take about 10 minutes. The haloumi will ooze lots of salty milky liquid before turning golden. Set aside.

Heat the olive oil in a frying pan and fry the red onion until it's beginning to brown. Add the garlic, chilli flakes and pink peppercorns and stir-fry for a couple of minutes.

Wash the spinach and rocket, steam, drain and set aside.

Cook the pasta following the instructions in cooking techniques on page 201. Don't add any salt as the haloumi is very salty.

In a large frying pan warm the onion mixture, add the wine, cream and yoghurt and simmer gently for a minute. Add the red pepper, haloumi and spinach/rocket mix and heat through.

Slowly add the pasta to the sauce until the proportions of pasta to sauce look right. You may not need all the pasta. Stir in, check for seasoning and add lots of freshly ground black pepper.

To serve

Serve with a tomato salad.

SERVES 4

2 large red peppers

250 g haloumi, cubed and dry-fried

1 tbsp olive oil

1 red onion, chopped

3 garlic cloves, finely chopped

1 tsp dried chilli flakes

1 tsp pink peppercorns, crushed

225 g young leaf spinach

50 g rocket

100 ml dry white wine

4 tbsps double cream

4 tbsps yoghurt

freshly ground black pepper

75 g to 100 g penne pasta per serving

Stir-fries

The Chinese word for stir-fry is 'chao' – hence 'chow mein'. The Chinese took this dish with them as their influence spread east to Japan and south through Vietnam, Laos, Cambodia and Thailand.

Cooking in a wok is fast, but stir-fries are not fast food. The key to a successful stir-fry is ensuring you have everything ready before you heat the wok. Have your vegetables sliced and in individual bowls, ensure the sauce is prepared and, most important of all, that the rice or noodles are cooked.

Colour and texture are all-important and this is easy to achieve as the vegetables are cooked quickly and so retain their colour and crispness. A stir-fry should be eaten as soon as it is cooked.

The best rice to use for stir-fries is a long grain Thai rice called fragrant or jasmine rice. It is slightly sticky when cooked and wonderfully aromatic.

Noodles are made with flour and water and sometimes egg. They can be used fresh or dried and can be eaten hot or cold. To really appreciate noodles, you hold the bowl near to your chin and slurp the noodles into your mouth. The louder the noise, the greater your appreciation of the food.

This is a sweet and sour Chinese dish, fresh and light but so different from those glutinous glutamate takeaways.

Chilli Sweet and Tangy Tofu
with Peppers

SERVES 4

285 g plain firm tofu, cut into 16 cubes

vegetable oil for shallow-frying

2 garlic cloves, finely chopped

1 tbsp sunflower oil

1 red, green and yellow pepper, cut into 2 cm chunks

2 large carrots, peeled and cut into slim rounds

6 spring onions, cut the white part into 2.5 cm lengths and thinly slice the best of the green for garnish

Sauce

2 tbsps sweet chilli sauce

2 tbsps tamari

1 tbsp tomato purée

1 tbsp white wine vinegar

1 tbsp sherry

1 tbsp soft brown sugar

150 ml vegetable stock

1 tsp cornflour, mixed to a paste with 1 tbsp of water

lots of freshly ground black pepper

medium egg noodles, enough for 4

Drain the tofu, cut into cubes and pat dry with kitchen paper. Heat the oil in a frying pan or wok. Add the cubes of tofu a few at a time and shallow-fry until golden and crisp, lift out with a slotted spoon and drain on kitchen paper.

Prepare the vegetables, keeping the carrots, peppers and spring onions in separate bowls. Keep the best of the green from the spring onions aside for a garnish.

Sauce

Mix the sauce ingredients together, except for the cornflour and black pepper.

Heat the wok, add the oil, when the oil is hot add the garlic and stir-fry until fragrant. Add the carrots and stir-fry for 1 minute. Add the peppers and stir-fry for a couple more minutes. Add the spring onions, white parts only, and stir-fry until all the vegetables are just tender. Add the fried tofu.

Pour in the sauce and bring to the boil, stirring all the time. Stir the cornflour paste into the sauce and simmer for 1 minute for the sauce to slightly thicken.

Drop the noodles into a large saucepan of boiling salted water, return to the boil and simmer for 4 minutes. Drain well and toss into the sauce.

To serve

Serve in individual bowls garnished with spring onion rings and freshly ground black pepper.

This stir-fry was so good we ate it every day whilst waiting in northern Thailand for visas. The combination of crunchy cashew nuts with the sweet peppery flavour of freshly picked green peppercorns was perfect.

Cashew Nut, Mock Chicken and Green Peppercorn Stir-fry

SERVES 4

350 g jar seitan (wheat gluten), drained and chopped

100 g whole cashew nuts

oil for deep-frying

3 carrots

2 green peppers

150 g mangetout peas

1 tbsp sunflower oil

Garlic Paste

6 garlic cloves, chopped

2 green chillies, finely sliced

2 lime leaves, shredded

1 lemongrass, peeled and finely sliced

Sauce

1 tbsp fresh green peppercorns

4 tbsps shoyu

1 tbsp tomato purée

1 tbsp lime juice

1 tsp kecap manis or brown sugar

handful of fresh chopped coriander

Thai fragrant rice, enough for 4

Deep-fry the cashew nuts, they will only need a minute as they burn very easily. Drain on kitchen paper.

Prepare the vegetables by peeling and slicing the carrots thinly on the angle, then cut the green pepper into chunks and the mangetout peas in half.

Garlic Paste

Whiz the garlic, chillies, lime leaves and lemongrass in a mini food processor to a smooth paste, or crush with a pestle and mortar.

Sauce

Mix the sauce ingredients together.

Heat the wok and add the oil. When the oil is hot, add the garlic paste and stir-fry until fragrant. Add the carrots and stir-fry for a minute, add the peppers and stir-fry for a couple more minutes, then add the cashew nuts, seitan and mangetout peas and stir-fry until just cooked, but still crisp. Stir in the sauce and toss the vegetables until hot.

Cook the Thai fragrant rice following the instructions in cooking techniques on page 201.

To serve

Garnish with freshly chopped coriander and serve with Thai fragrant rice.

Seitan is wheat gluten. It's vegan and very high in protein – see page 194.

♦ VEGAN ♦

Haloumi is a Middle Eastern semi-hard cheese. It's a great addition to stir-fries, where its crisp saltiness contrasts superbly with the spring greenness of the vegetables.

Haloumi, Green Vegetable Stir-fry
with Coriander and Lemongrass

In a non-stick frying pan fry the haloumi cubes without oil until they are golden all over. The haloumi will exude a milky salty whey before turning golden.

Finely chop the garlic, chillies and lemon grass or whiz in a mini processor.

Prepare all the vegetables and put each variety into a separate bowl.

Heat up a wok and add the oil and then the garlic, chilli and lemongrass paste. Stir-fry these until fragrant, but make sure the garlic does not burn.

Add the vegetables, courgettes first, then the green pepper, mushrooms and lastly the mangetout peas, stir-fry for a couple of minutes between each variety. Add the fried haloumi to the vegetables.

Mix the tamari with the apple juice concentrate, lime zest and juice, pour over the vegetables and quickly stir-fry.

Cook the Thai fragrant rice following the instructions in cooking techniques on page 201.

To serve

Mix the coriander into the stir-fry, leaving a little for garnish, and serve at once with Thai fragrant rice.

SERVES 4

250 g haloumi, cubed

2 tbsps sunflower oil

4 garlic cloves

2 green chillies

I stick lemongrass

2 small courgettes, sliced

I green pepper, sliced

150 g button mushrooms

150 g mangetout peas, topped and tailed

I tbsp tamari

I tsp apple juice concentrate

I lime, zest and juice

handful of fresh coriander, chopped

Thai fragrant rice, enough for 4

This is a chilli-hot Laotian stir-fry with a sweet finish, traditionally made with beef, for which we substitute tempeh.

Hot Red Pepper Tempeh Stir-Fry
with Flat Rice Noodles

SERVES 4

220 g tempeh

oil for shallow-frying

2 tbsps sunflower oil

2 shallots, thinly sliced

3 garlic cloves, chopped

1 large red chilli, thinly sliced

1 red pepper, sliced

Sauce

1 tbsp tamari

3 tbsps demerera sugar

1 tbsp tamarind pulp or 1 tsp tamarind concentrate

2 tbsps water

flat rice noodles, enough for 4

fresh coriander, chopped

Cut the tempeh into thick matchsticks and shallow-fry, until crisp and golden. Drain on kitchen paper.

Heat the wok and add the oil. When it's hot, add the shallots and stir-fry for a minute. Add the garlic and chilli and quickly stir-fry these, then add the red pepper and stir-fry for a couple more minutes. Finally, add the tempeh.

Sauce

Make up the sauce by combining the ingredients in a bowl.

Stir the sauce into the stir-fry and cook over a high heat, tossing the tempeh mix until the sauce begins to caramelise and becomes thick and glossy.

Place the noodles in a large bowl, cover with boiling water and leave to stand for 4 minutes. Drain and serve.

To serve

Pile the noodles on plates, spoon on the stir-fry and garnish with fresh, chopped coriander.

Tempeh comes from Indonesia and is made of compressed, lightly fermented soya beans. Packed full of protein, it is free from cholesterol and has a delicious nutty flavour and chewy texture.

♦ VEGAN ♦

Guy's stir-fry is easy to make and served with a rich Japanese teriyaki sauce. Guy has been a chef at Demuths for the past eight years and loves making stir-fries

Guy's Super-Duper Tofu Stir-fry
with Jasmine Fragrant Rice Flavoured with Coriander and Lime

Teriyaki Marinade

Make up the teriyaki marinade by pouring all the ingredients into a small saucepan, bringing to the boil and simmering very gently for 5 minutes. Pour the hot marinade over the tofu strips and leave to marinate for 30 minutes.

Stir-fry Vegetables

Prepare the vegetables for the stir-fry. When you are ready to cook, strain the marinade from the tofu into a saucepan and simmer until the teriyaki sauce is reduced by a third. Lightly fry the tofu in the sunflower oil until crisp.

Cook the jasmine fragrant rice following the instructions in cooking techniques on page 201. When cooked mix in the chopped coriander, zest of a lime and a pinch of salt.

Heat the wok, add the toasted sesame oil and when hot add the red onion and stir-fry this quickly over a high heat.

Add the green beans and toss for a minute, then add the rest of the vegetables and stir-fry until just tender, but still with a crisp bite. Add the lime juice and stir in.

To serve

Serve at once. Place a circle of rice on the serving dish, then pile on the steaming hot vegetables, top with the lightly fried tofu and drizzle with teriyaki sauce.

Sake is Japanese rice wine. You can substitute it with medium white wine. Mirin is a Japanese sweet wine used almost exclusively for cooking. You can substitute sweet sherry, but it has a rather strong flavour.

SERVES 4

250 g plain tofu, cut into 5 cm strips

4 tbsps sunflower oil for frying

Teriyaki Marinade

100 ml apple juice

50 ml sake or white wine

1 tbsp tamari

1 tbsp mirin or sweet sherry

1 tbsp apple juice concentrate or brown sugar

thumb of ginger, grated, with the juice squeezed out

1 red chilli, halved and deseeded

Stir-fry Vegetables

1 tbsp toasted sesame oil

1 small red onion finely sliced

100 g green beans, topped, tailed and halved

100 g baby corn, sliced lengthways

1 red pepper, sliced thinly

1 orange pepper, sliced thinly

juice of a lime

jasmine fragrant rice, for 4

handful fresh coriander, chopped

zest of 1 lime

pinch of salt

◆ **VEGAN** ◆

MAIN DISHES

Comfort Food 62

For those dark autumn and winter nights when you need reassurance and warmth

Rich Dishes 76

More complex recipes which need time to prepare

Chilli Meals 110

Curried, chilli and hot dishes that can set your palate and mind on fire

Comfort Food

These recipes are comforting, sustaining, reassuring and warming. Comfort food is one area where the British excel and these recipes have their place on cold, dark autumn and winter evenings, when you are drawn towards earthy and muted foods such as the sweetness of butternut squash and the inky richness of mushrooms. Food at this time of the year should be rich, piping hot and comforting.

These are dishes that require long, slow cooking, maybe in organic ale, or they are thick, tasty stews, perhaps full of plump dumplings or hearty robust rice dishes.

Most of these recipes taste best when served in large deep bowls that you can eat on your knees in front of a blazing fire.

They can be made in large quantities for freezing and storing and are best accompanied by a mound of creamy potatoes, mashed with butter and topped with a big dollop of crème fraîche. Nothing low fat – it's not a time to be watching the calories.

Bangers and mash are the ultimate in comfort food and sometimes even chips can sneak in, when cut thick, rolled in chilli, quickly fried and then dipped into a thick yoghurt dip.

Kedgeree is a colonial adaptation of the Indian dish khichhari, made with rice and lentils and served with khuri, a sour milk sauce, poppadoms and chutney. This is a scrumptious vegetarian version that has the bonus of not stinking the kitchen with fish smells.

Vedgeree
with Poppadoms and Tomato and Papaya Chutney

SERVES 4

275 g basmati rice

3 eggs, hardboiled and chopped

25 g butter

1 onion, finely chopped

2 garlic cloves, chopped

1 tsp curry powder

1/2 tsp turmeric

1/2 tsp chilli powder

150 g oyster mushrooms, shredded

200 g frozen organic peas

150 g smoked cheese, diced

lots of fresh chopped parsley

salt and fresh black pepper

25 g flaked almonds, toasted

Tomato and Papaya Chutney

3 cm piece root ginger

2 garlic cloves, peeled

1 red chilli, finely sliced

1 tbsp sunflower oil

1 tsp punch puran

700 g tomatoes, cored and chopped

50 g dried apricots, chopped

100 g soft brown sugar

100 ml wine vinegar

1/4 tsp salt

1/2 small papaya

Making vedgeree involves a number of different tasks; cooking the rice, hardboiling the eggs, frying the onions and toasting the almonds before everything is mixed together.

Measure the rice into a measuring jug as you'll need 1 part water to 1 part rice. Rinse the rice until the water runs clear and place in a medium saucepan with a tight fitting lid. Add the measured water, which should just cover the rice. Cover and bring to the boil, then turn down the heat and simmer until all the water is absorbed – should take about 5 minutes. Take off the heat and leave to stand covered for a further 5 minutes.

Fry the onion in the butter until translucent but not browned, add the garlic and spices and stir-fry. Add the oyster mushrooms and cook for 5 minutes. Then add the peas and cook until tender.

Mix in the cooked rice, diced smoked cheese, chopped boiled eggs and parsley. Season with salt and freshly ground black pepper.

Tomato and Papaya Chutney

Peel and chop the ginger and then whiz this, together with the garlic and chilli, in a mini food processor, to a chunky paste. Heat the sunflower oil in a large saucepan, add the ginger mix and the punch puran and stir-fry until fragrant.

Add the tomatoes, apricots, sugar, vinegar and salt, stir and simmer gently for 30 minutes until it has reduced to a thick chutney consistency. Peel and chop the papaya, add this to the mixture and simmer for 5 minutes. Leave to cool.

To serve

Serve the vedgeree hot, sprinkled with toasted almonds and accompanied by poppadoms and Tomato and Papaya Chutney.

Stews and slow-cooking dishes have become fashionable again and are perfect for cold winter days. The tasty herb and mustard dumplings that accompany this stew are the ultimate in comfort food.

Root Vegetable Stew
with Herb and Mustard Dumplings and Garlic Mash

SERVES 4

6 shallots, peeled and quartered

4 tbsps olive oil

2 garlic cloves, finely chopped

1 leek, sliced

2 large carrots, peeled and chopped

1 parsnip, peeled and chopped

1 turnip, peeled and chopped

2 potatoes, peeled and cut into chunks

440 ml organic cider

1 tbsp sherry

2 bay leaves

a few sage leaves

500 ml boiling water

1 tbsp tamari

1 tsp Marmite

1 tsp vegetable bouillon powder

salt and freshly ground black pepper

handful of fresh parsley, chopped

In a large casserole dish fry the shallots in the olive oil until they are golden. Add the garlic and leeks and fry for a couple more minutes. Then add the carrots, parsnip, turnip and potatoes and stir-fry. Add the cider and sherry and bring to the boil.

Mix the tamari, Marmite and bouillon into the boiling water and add this to the stew, along with the bay and sage leaves. Season to taste and simmer gently for about 30 minutes or until all the vegetables are nearly cooked.

Herb and Mustard Dumplings

While the stew is simmering make the dumplings. They need to be added 15 minutes before the stew is ready.

Sieve the flour with the mustard powder into a large bowl, then add the vegetable suet, fresh herbs, salt and freshly ground black pepper. Just before adding to the stew, mix in enough water, a little at a time, to make a firm but not sticky dough. With floured hands, break the dough into about 12 small pieces and roll them into round dumplings.

Check the stew for seasoning and add the freshly chopped parsley. Then add the dumplings, pushing them down into the liquid. Simmer gently for 15 minutes or until the dumplings have doubled in size.

The choice of vegetables can be varied according to your preferences and to what you have available. If you like swede, add some, and if you don't like turnip, leave it out.

Garlic Mash

To make Garlic Mash, sauté 4 chopped garlic cloves in margarine, and then add the boiled potatoes and mash.

To serve

Serve the stew with Garlic Mash and steamed sprouts.

Herb and Mustard Dumplings

110 g self-raising white flour

1 tsp mustard powder

50 g vegetable suet

1 tbsp chopped fresh parsley

½ tbsp chopped fresh sage

salt and freshly ground black pepper

cold water to mix

Garlic Mash

4 large potatoes

4 garlic cloves, chopped

25 g vegan margarine

This is a 19th century Welsh recipe for skinless meatless sausages, popular when it was the norm for towns to have their own local sausages. During the Second World War the recipe was revived because of rationing.

Glamorgan Sausages
with Rich Onion Gravy and Pesto Mash

SERVES 4

150 g organic wholewheat breadcrumbs

150 g strong Cheddar cheese, grated

6 spring onions, finely sliced with the best of the green

2 tbsps fresh parsley, chopped

1 tbsp fresh sage, chopped

1 tsp vegetable bouillon powder

1 tsp mustard powder

1/2 tsp paprika

freshly ground black pepper

2 egg yolks (keep the whites)

polenta for rolling the sausages

2 egg whites

sunflower oil for frying

Rich Onion Gravy

1 large onion, finely sliced

1 tbsp sunflower oil

1 tsp Marmite

250 ml hot water

1 tbsp plain white flour

salt and freshly ground black pepper

Pesto Mash

4 large potatoes

1 tbsp pesto

Whiz up the bread in a food processor. Add the cheese, spring onions, parsley, sage, bouillon powder, mustard, paprika, salt and pepper and whiz again. Then add the egg yolks and mix. The consistency should be soft and malleable, but not sticky.

Divide the mixture into 8 similar sized pieces and roll each one into a thin sausage, about 8 cm long. Dip the sausages in egg white and then roll them in the polenta. Shallow-fry in sunflower oil until crisp and golden.

Rich Onion Gravy

Gently fry the onion in the sunflower oil until soft, but not browned. Take off the heat and set aside.

Place the Marmite in a measuring jug and pour in the hot water, stir until the Marmite has dissolved.

Reheat the onions and stir in the flour and, on a medium heat, slowly add the hot water and Marmite, stirring all the time. Simmer for a few minutes until the gravy has thickened and season to taste with salt and black pepper.

Pesto Mash

For pesto mash, just stir in a tablespoon of pesto to mashed potato before serving.

To serve

Serve the sausages on a mound of pesto mashed potatoes, accompanied by the gravy and grilled tomatoes. For a festive touch this dish is delicious with cranberry relish – see page 185.

Carbonade of beef was one of my mother's favourite dishes. My vegetarian version is made with firm organic chestnut mushrooms, seitan and organic ale. The quantities look huge, but it cooks down by half and is even better the next day.

Chestnut Mushroom and Seitan Carbonade

SERVES 4/6

4 medium onions, sliced

4 tbsps olive oil

4 garlic cloves, finely chopped

500 g chestnut mushrooms, quartered

350 g jar 'Yakso' seitan

1 tbsp plain white flour

1 teaspoon vegetable bouillon powder

1 teaspoon Marmite

1 tbsp shoyu

500 ml boiling water

500 ml organic pale ale

2 bay leaves

1 tbsp brown sugar

salt and freshly ground black pepper

slices of brown bread

French mustard

Pre-heat the oven to 190°C/Gas 5.

Heat the olive oil in a large ovenproof casserole dish. Add the sliced onions and fry until golden and beginning to caramelise. Then add the garlic and fry for a further minute.

Add the quartered mushrooms, turn up the heat and stir-fry until the mushrooms are beginning to brown.

Cut the seitan into chunks, keeping the liquid from the jar to add to the stock. Add the seitan to the mushrooms and stir-fry quickly. Take the casserole off the heat and stir in the flour.

Make the stock with the bouillon, Marmite, shoyu and the liquid from the seitan jar and make up to 500 ml with boiling water.

Over a low heat, stir the stock into the casserole and then add the beer, bay leaves and sugar. Bring to the boil, stirring all the time. Lower the heat and simmer very gently for about 30 minutes until the carbonade has reduced by 1/3rd and is a lovely rich brown colour. Check for seasoning and add salt and lots of freshly ground black pepper.

Slice enough bread to cover the top of the casserole, spreading it with a generous amount of French mustard. Place the slices, mustard side up, so that they cover the carbonade. Push the bread down into the gravy. It's essential that there is enough liquid for you to be able to dunk the bread. If not, add a little more boiling water to the stew before adding the bread.

Place the casserole in the oven and cook for 30 mintutes or until the bread is crisp and golden.

To serve

Serve with creamy mashed potato and purple sprouting broccoli.

Paella is a Spanish savoury mixture of rice, vegetables and traditionally anything meaty or fishy that is in season. It is cooked in a large shallow paellera pan over a charcoal fire. The pan is then placed in the centre of the table and everyone eats straight from it.

Pepper and Green Bean Paella
with Chickpeas

In a large deep frying pan, fry the onion in the olive oil until soft and translucent, add the garlic and stir-fry for 5 minutes.

Add the sliced peppers and the paprika, stir well and cook for a further 5 minutes. Stir in the rice and mix well to coat the grains.

Add the diced tomatoes, blanched green beans, drained chickpeas, bay leaf, fresh thyme, saffron, sherry and dry white wine. Simmer for a few minutes until all the liquid has been absorbed.

Add the stock, bring to the boil and simmer very gently for 15 minutes, stirring occasionally to prevent the mixture sticking. If your frying pan is not big enough, decant the mixture into a large flat, ovenproof dish. Stir in the stock, cover with silver foil and bake in the oven at 200°C/Gas 6 for 15 minutes or until the rice is cooked and has absorbed all the stock.

Season with salt and freshly ground black pepper and add the parsley.

To serve

Serve paella the Spanish way, straight from the frying pan.

Spanish rice is not as starchy as risotto rice. The best paella rice is grown in Valencia. When cooked it should be fluffy and the grains separate.

If you can't find paella rice, organic white long grain rice is a good alternative. If you use risotto rice you will end up with a creamy rice dish, delicious but more like a risotto than a paella.

SERVES 4/6

250 g Spanish paella rice

4 tbsps olive oil

1 medium onion, chopped

2 garlic cloves, finely chopped

1 yellow pepper, sliced into matchsticks

1 red pepper, sliced into matchsticks

2 tsps paprika

6 fresh tomatoes, diced small, cores cut out

100 g green beans, topped and tailed, cut in half and blanched

425 g tin of sugar free chickpeas, drained and rinsed

1 bay leaf

1 tbsp fresh thyme leaves

1 large pinch saffron threads, infused in hot water

100 ml dry sherry

100 ml dry white wine

570 ml vegetable stock, made with 1 tsp vegetable bouillon powder

salt and freshly ground black pepper

handful of fresh parsley, chopped

♦ VEGAN ♦

This is a light, bright spring casserole, ideal for a quick, filling meal.
It is served with Patatas Bravas – Spanish chilli potatoes.

Vegetable and Bean Frenzy
with Patatas Bravas

SERVES 4

400 g tin flageolet beans, drained and rinsed

1 onion, sliced

3 tbsps olive oil

2 garlic cloves, finely chopped

1 green pepper, sliced

1 red pepper, sliced

1 stick celery, chopped

1/2 fennel bulb, sliced

250 ml white wine

1 tbsp apple juice concentrate

1 tbsp lemon juice

1/2 tsp fennel seeds

1 tsp vegetable bouillon powder

1 tbsp fresh thyme

salt and freshly ground black pepper

water to cover

handful of freshly chopped parsley

Patatas Bravas

1 kilo organic potatoes, peeled and sliced into wedges

olive oil for roasting

1 tbsp paprika

1 tbsp cayenne

salt

In a large casserole fry the onion in the olive oil until soft. Add the garlic and fry for a couple more minutes. Then add the peppers, celery and fennel and stir-fry for 5 minutes.

Finally, add the flageolet beans, wine, apple juice concentrate, lemon juice, fennel seeds, bouillon and thyme. Pour in enough water to cover, and season with salt and freshly ground black pepper. Bring to the boil, turn down the heat and simmer gently for 15 minutes.

Stir in a handful of freshly chopped parsley and check for flavour.

Patatas Bravas

Pre-heat the oven to 225°C/Gas 7.

Add enough olive oil to cover a large roasting tin and place this in the pre-heated oven for 5 minutes to heat up the oil. Stir the spices into the hot oil, add the potato wedges and stir so that the potatoes are covered in the spicy oil.

Roast until golden, stirring once or twice during the cooking to stop the potatoes sticking.

Drain on kitchen paper, sprinkle with sea salt and serve at once.

To serve

Serve the Vegetable Bean Frenzy hot, in large soup bowls, accompanied by the Patatas Bravas and a dollop of sour cream.

◆ VEGAN ◆

Rich Dishes

I'm a great advocate of eating, wherever possible, vegetables in season as well as from the area and the country that you are living in. Flying asparagus around the globe to satisfy supposed cravings for it in mid-winter is madness.

Our bodies, if left to their own devices, will tend to choose the right vegetables at the right time of year.

In the following recipes you will find a selection for each season. They tend to be more complex to follow than others in this book. Although simple to make, only choose them when you have lots of time, as they are invariably made up of a number of different elements. They are ideal for celebrations, dinner parties, birthdays and Christmas.

They use copious amounts of fresh herbs and a number of them have alcohol in them. Try using organic vegan wine and sherry, it can make a subtle difference.

They tend to be of Mediterranean style except for the Iranian aubergines and the teriyaki tofu. Most come with sauces and are without exception extremely filling. They are rich in taste and colour but there is still lots of choice for vegans.

A very light, early summer dish with sweet thin-skinned romano peppers, asparagus and toasted almonds. It is served with a delicious herb-packed salsa verde.

Sweet Romano Peppers
Stuffed with Quinoa and Asparagus

SERVES 4

4 sweet romano red peppers

50 g quinoa, very well washed

1 tsp Marmite

4 garlic cloves, finely chopped

1 red chilli, finely sliced

2 tbsps olive oil

50 g carrots, grated

75 g courgettes, grated

4 spring onions, diced

25 g flaked almonds, toasted

100 g asparagus

1 tsp paprika

2 tbsps lemon juice

1 tbsp tamari

1 tbsp apple juice concentrate

handful of flat leaf parsley, chopped

salt and freshly ground black pepper

Quinoa is a tiny golden seed from South America. Cultivated since 3000 BC, it has higher protein content than rice and is gluten-free.

Pre-heat the oven to 200°C/Gas 6.

Place the quinoa and Marmite in a saucepan and cover with plenty of water, bring to the boil and then simmer for 10–15 minutes. Drain and set aside.

Wok-fry the garlic and the chilli in the olive oil until fragrant. Add the grated carrots, courgettes and spring onions and stir-fry until the carrots are soft and the cooking juices have evaporated.

Toast the flaked almonds until golden.

To cook the asparagus, peel the bottom part of the stems, discarding any woody bits. Reserve the tips and dice the rest. Boil the diced stems until soft and steam the tips in a sieve over the pan or in the top of a steamer.

In a large bowl mix all the ingredients except for the asparagus tips, which should be kept for decoration. Check for seasoning.

Slice the peppers lengthways and remove the seeds and pith. Under a hot grill slightly roast the peppers, outer side up, until they begin to blister, but before they go black.

Oil an ovenproof dish large enough to hold the peppers. Fill the peppers with the quinoa mix and bake in the pre-heated oven for 20 minutes.

To serve

Serve drizzled with salsa verde (see page 188), a green leaf salad and decorate with the asparagus tips.

Rösti originated in Switzerland and is always made with grated par-boiled potatoes. Our version is made with sweet potato – for its sweetness and colour – and is piled high with warming winter vegetables in a rich, organic sherry marinade.

Sweet Potato Rösti
with Braised Vegetables in an Organic Sherry Marinade

SERVES 4

400 g sweet potatoes, peeled

400 g waxy potatoes, peeled

1 tbsp fresh rosemary

1 tbsp fresh thyme

pinch of salt and freshly ground black pepper

olive oil for frying

Braised Vegetables

50 ml olive oil

100 g shallots, peeled and halved

100 g carrots, peeled and sliced thickly

100 g leeks, sliced

6 garlic cloves, peeled and left whole

100 g green pepper, sliced

150 g marrow, cut in chunks

2 bay leaves

1 red chilli, finely chopped

You will need 4 x 10 cm scone/muffin rings to fry the rösti in.

Cut the peeled potatoes into large chunks. Par-boil the sweet potatoes and ordinary potatoes separately, as the sweet potatoes cook more quickly. Leave to cool, as they are much easier to grate when cool.

Grate both types of potato and mix together.

Prepare the herbs by removing the stalks and chopping finely. Add these to the potato mix, season with salt and freshly ground black pepper and mix in well.

Heat 1 tablespoon of olive oil in a large non-stick frying pan and brush olive oil around the inside of each scone ring. Place the scone rings in the frying pan and fill with rösti mix. Press down and fry gently on one side for 10 minutes, then turn over and cook the other side for a further 10 minutes, until they are golden on both sides.

Leave the rösti to firm up and cool slightly, then slide a sharp knife around the inside of the scone ring and gently remove them. Place on a dish and keep warm.

Braised Vegetables

Pre-heat the oven to 200°C/Gas 6.

Heat the olive oil in a large baking tin and add the shallots, carrots, leeks and garlic. Cover with silver foil and braise for 15 minutes.

Then add the green pepper, marrow, bay leaves and red chilli and stir well. Replace the foil and braise for a further 15 minutes.

Finally, take off the silver foil and roast for another 10 minutes or until the vegetables are golden and beginning to caramelise.

Organic Sherry Marinade

In a saucepan, combine the water, tamari, tomato purée, bouillon, apple juice concentrate, Marmite and sherry. Bring to the boil and then simmer until reduced by half – this should take about 10 minutes.

Add the diced tomatoes, 1 tablespoon of the fresh herbs and lots of freshly ground black pepper and simmer for 5 minutes.

To serve

Serve the rösti piled high with braised vegetables and with the hot Organic Sherry Marinade spooned over. Decorate with the remaining fresh herbs.

Organic Sherry Marinade

250 ml boiling water

1 tbsp tamari

1 tbsp tomato purée

1 tsp vegetable bouillon powder

1 tsp apple juice concentrate

½ tsp Marmite

50 ml organic sherry

150 g fresh tomatoes, peeled, deseeded and finely diced

2 tbsps chopped fresh herbs

freshly ground black pepper

This aubergine dish is typically Iranian, with a mix of sweet and savoury ingredients flavoured with aromatic spices more commonly used in puddings.

Iranian Stuffed Aubergines
with a Coconut and Almond Sauce

SERVES 6

3 medium aubergines

1 medium onion, finely chopped

1 tbsp olive oil

4 garlic cloves, chopped

1 red chilli, finely sliced

1 green pepper, diced

50 ml orange juice

100 g chickpeas, cooked weight

150 g roasted cashews

100 g dried apricots

100 g dates, chopped

2 tomatoes, diced

1 tbsp lemon juice

handful of fresh coriander, chopped

salt and lots of freshly ground black pepper

Spice Mix

1 tsp cumin

1 tsp cinnamon

1 tsp ground ginger

1/2 tsp ground nutmeg

1/2 tsp turmeric

Pre-heat the oven to 200°C/Gas 6.

Cut the aubergines in half lengthways and place them on a roasting tray, cut side uppermost. Cover with silver foil and roast in the pre-heated oven until soft and cooked through – about 30 minutes. Leave the aubergines to cool and then scoop out the middles leaving enough flesh for support. Coarsely chop the insides of the aubergines and set aside.

Rehydrate the apricots in boiling water for 30 minutes and then chop finely.

Spice Mix

Make up the spice mix by combining all the ingredients in a bowl.

Fry the onion in the olive oil until translucent, add the garlic and chilli and stir-fry for a couple of minutes. Add the spice mix and stir-fry until fragrant, then add the green pepper and orange juice. Stir well and simmer until the green pepper is soft.

Roast or toast the cashews taking care that they don't burn. Mix the cashews with the cooked chickpeas, chopped apricots, chopped dates and diced tomatoes.

Add the cashew mix to the onion spice mix along with the chopped aubergine insides, lemon juice, coriander, salt and lots of black pepper. Reserve some coriander for the garnish.

Oil an ovenproof dish and pile the filling into the aubergine skins and bake in the pre-heated oven for 30 minutes.

Coconut and Almond Sauce

Gently fry the onion in the margarine until soft, add the garlic and ginger and fry very gently. Make sure the onion and garlic don't brown, as this will ruin the colour of the sauce.

Add the spices to the onion mixture and then add the coconut milk, water and cinnamon stick. Bring to the boil and simmer gently for 15 minutes.

Take off the heat and remove the cinnamon stick. Add the ground almonds, lime zest, lime juice and a pinch of salt. Blend the sauce in a liquidiser and check for seasoning.

To serve

Garnish the stuffed aubergines with fresh coriander and serve with the Coconut and Almond Sauce and a green salad.

Coconut and Almond Sauce

1 tbsp sunflower margarine

1 small onion, chopped

2 garlic cloves, chopped

2 cm ginger, peeled and finely chopped

1 tsp turmeric

$1/2$ tsp cayenne

400 ml coconut milk

750 ml water

1 cinnamon stick

100 g ground almonds

zest and juice of $1/2$ lime

salt

Blini are small Russian pancakes, traditionally made with buckwheat flour leavened with yeast and eaten with butter or, more famously, with caviar and sour cream. These pumpkin blini are a fantastic orange colour and much lighter than traditional ones.

Pumpkin Blini Stack
with Mushroom and Bean Filling, and Wine and Herb Sauce

SERVES 4

300 g pumpkin or squash, peeled and deseeded

75 g plain flour, sieved

2 eggs, separated

250 ml milk

pinch of salt

Choose a pumpkin or squash with a bright orange flesh to give the blini a vibrant colour. Peel, deseed and chop up the pumpkin and cook till tender but not mushy. Drain, leave to cool and then purée.

Mix the flour with the puréed pumpkin and the beaten egg yolks. Slowly whisk in 250 ml milk to make a thick consistency and season with a pinch of salt.

Whisk the egg whites till they form soft peaks, but are not as firm as you need for meringues. Fold them into the blini batter, ensuring an even consistency with no blobs of egg white floating around.

Gently heat a frying pan or griddle and brush with sunflower oil. Pour in a small ladle full of batter, enough to make a 1/2 cm thick pancake approx 10 cm in diameter.

Fry the blini gently on one side until they are golden. Then flip them over and do the same on the other side. Make sure they don't brown, as this will ruin the delicate flavour.

This mix will make about 12 blini, enough for 3 per person.

Shiitake mushrooms or tree mushrooms grow on tree trunks and have a strong earthy flavour and are high in protein.

Oyster mushrooms also grow on trees and are bluey-white, look rather like oyster shells and even have a fishy flavour.

Smelling of apricots, chanterelles/girolles are golden yellow, shaped like a trumpet and are one of the most fragrant and delicate of the wild mushrooms.

Mushroom and Bean Filling

250 g shallots, peeled and roughly chopped

6 garlic cloves, peeled and sliced lengthways

3 tbsps extra virgin olive oil

300 g chestnut mushrooms, cut in quarters

100 g chanterelles, left whole

100 g shiitake mushrooms, left whole

100 g oyster mushrooms, left whole

250 g green beans

1 tbsp shoyu

4 tbsps fresh chopped herbs, chives, parsley, basil and oregano

salt and lots of freshly ground black pepper.

Wine and Herb Sauce

150 ml white wine

100 ml water

4 tbsps cream

2 tbsps fresh chopped herbs

salt and freshly ground black pepper

Mushroom and Bean Filling

Prepare the chanterelles by picking off any moss or leaves, cut off the roots and gently brush with a mushroom or pastry brush to remove any dirt. Seal in the flavour of the chanterelles by dry-frying them in a frying pan with no oil until they begin to exude juices. Set aside.

Heat the olive oil in a large frying pan or wok. Add the shallots and stir-fry on a low heat for at least 5 minutes or until golden.

Add the garlic and stir-fry for a minute. Toss in all the mushrooms, stir so that they are well covered in oil and then cook gently until they are tender.

Top and tail the green beans, cut in half, and blanch for 5 minutes. Add the blanched green beans, shoyu and fresh herbs to the mushroom mix and stir-fry gently for a couple of minutes. Season with salt and lots of black pepper.

Wine and Herb Sauce

In a small saucepan heat the white wine and water and simmer for 5 minutes. Add the cream and heat gently, then add the herbs and season to taste. The sauce should be thin.

To serve

Make sure that your blini are warm, the filling and sauce are hot and the plates are warmed. Place a blini in the middle of each plate and spoon on a couple of tablespoons of Mushroom and Bean Filling. Cover with the next blini, add more filling, another blini and finally a little more filling on top, artistically placed. Pour the White Wine and Herb Sauce around the blini stack and serve with seasonal vegetables.

These stuffed onions make a warming winter dish and the Scottish twist makes them ideal for a Burns Night supper.

Oatmeal and Whisky Stuffed Onions
with a Cracked Black Pepper and Cream Sauce

Pre-heat the oven to190°C/Gas 5.

To prepare the onions, cut a sliver from the bottom of each onion, so that they can stand upright. Cut a cross in the top to about ¾ of the way down the onions. Place them in a large pan, cover with cold water and bring to the boil. Simmer for 15 minutes, drain and refresh the onions under cold water.

Cut out the centres of the onions leaving the skin and 3 or 4 outer onion layers intact. Save three onion centres for the filling. Keep the rest to use in soup.

To make the stuffing, boil the green lentils in plenty of water until tender. Drain and set aside. Melt half the margarine in a saucepan, add the oats and oatmeal, stir in and cook very gently for a few minutes until the oats are toasted and golden.

Melt the rest of the margarine in another saucepan, add the carrots, onion and mushrooms and sauté until they have softened. Take off the heat and stir in the toasted oats, cooked lentils, vegetable suet, whisky, Marmite, herbs and spices. Season to taste.

Fill the onions with the stuffing and tie up with string to stop them falling apart. Place them in a roasting tin, wedging them in so that they don't fall over. Roast in the pre-heated oven for 40 minutes.

To make the sauce, gently heat the cream and stir in the cracked black pepper.

To serve

Serve in their skins, which will have baked to a beautiful golden colour, just don't eat them! with the cracked black pepper cream sauce and traditional Scottish mashed neeps (turnips) and tatties (potatoes).

SERVES 6

6 medium unpeeled brown-skinned onions

75 g margarine

50 g rolled oats

50 g pinhead oatmeal

100 g Cheddar

insides of 3 onions, finely chopped

100 g mushrooms, finely chopped

1 medium carrot, finely chopped

50 g green lentils

50 g vegetable suet

25 ml whisky

1 tsp Marmite

2 tbsps chopped mixed fresh herbs

pinch of nutmeg

dash of Tabasco

salt and freshly ground black pepper

250 ml single cream

1 tsp cracked black pepper

We serve these soufflés in December in the run-up to Christmas. They are creamy-white with a hint of blue from the Stilton, topped with walnuts and served with a rich, slightly sweet courgette, apple and mushroom sauce.

Stilton and Potato Soufflés
with Courgette, Apple and Mushroom Sauce

Pre-heat the oven to 190°C/Gas 5.

You'll need 6 x 10 cm scone/muffin rings to cook the soufflés in.

Par-boil the potatoes and leave them to cool, as they are much easier to grate when cold. Grate the potatoes and Stilton and mix these in with the spring onions, yoghurt, salt and pepper. Check for seasoning. Beat the egg yolks and mix them into the potato mixture. Then whisk the egg whites into firm peaks and fold them into the mixture with a metal spoon.

Oil the insides of the scone rings. Line a baking tray with parchment and place the oiled scone rings on the tray. Spoon the potato mix into the rings to half full and sprinkle with crushed walnuts.

Bake in the middle of the pre-heated oven for 20 minutes until the soufflés have puffed up and are golden on top. Check they are cooked through by piercing with a skewer. If the skewer comes out clean they are cooked through.

Lift on to a wire cooling tray and leave to cool a little. Then slide a sharp knife around the insides of the rings and gently remove them.

Courgette, Apple and Mushroom Sauce

Gently fry the onion in the olive oil until soft, but not browned. Add the courgettes and mushrooms and fry gently for a few minutes.

Pour in the white wine and reduce the sauce by a third. Add the sliced apple and cream and simmer for 5 minutes.

Add the fresh dill and season with salt and fresh black pepper.

To serve

Serve warm with Courgette, Apple and Mushroom Sauce.

SERVES 6

300 g floury potatoes, peeled and quartered

100 g Stilton, grated

4 spring onions, finely chopped

200 g Greek-style yoghurt

salt and freshly ground black pepper

6 eggs, separated

25 g walnuts, crushed

Courgette, Apple and Mushroom Sauce

1 onion, finely sliced

1 tablespoon olive oil

1 medium courgette, cut in thick moon shapes

100 g closed cup mushrooms, thickly sliced

75 ml white wine

1 green eating apple, cored and sliced in moon shapes

50 ml cream

salt and freshly ground black pepper

fresh dill, chopped and lots of it

Teriyaki sauce is a sweet, flavoursome Japanese soya sauce.
To 'teriyaki' is to marinate in teriyaki sauce and then to
cook, basted with the sauce, until the sauce is
reduced to a sweet, rich, glossy brown.

Teriyaki Tofu with Char-grilled Vegetables
Wasabi and Sesame Noodles, and Stir-fried Pak Choy

SERVES 4

285 g plain tofu

Teriyaki Marinade

2 tbsps tamari

2 tbsps mirin or sweet sherry

2 tbsps apple juice concentrate

2 tbsps water

1 tbsp ginger juice

1 large red pepper

1 large yellow pepper

1 large aubergine

2 tbsps sunflower oil

Wasabi is a Japanese condiment paste with a luminous bright green colour. It is also known as Japanese horseradish. Even though it is not related to horseradish it does have a similar fiery flavour and can bring tears to the eyes! Wasabi is usually eaten as a condiment with sushi.

Pre-heat the oven to 200°C/Gas 6.

Drain the tofu and press under a heavy weight for 1 hour. I find the easiest way to do this is to put the tofu between two chopping boards with a heavy weight on top. Place some kitchen roll underneath the chopping board to soak up the water from the tofu.

Cut the pressed tofu into two slim slices from top to bottom and then cut each slice into four.

Teriyaki Marinade

Make up the marinade by mixing the ingredients together in a bowl. Add the tofu and marinate for 30 minutes, turning it a couple of times so that it's evenly coated.

Cut the peppers in half and remove the seeds. Roast under a hot grill, topside uppermost, until blistered and charred. Leave to cool and then peel off the burned skin. Cut each half into two so that you end up with 8 pieces of pepper.

Cut the aubergine into 8 thick slices and fry in 1 tablespoon of sunflower oil until golden. Set aside.

Take the tofu out of the marinade and fry it in the remainder of the oil until tanned. Keep the marinade to serve with the finished dish.

Oil an ovenproof dish and place 4 aubergine slices in the bottom. Top each aubergine slice with a slice of pepper, then aubergine, then pepper and finish with the tofu. Pour over half the marinade and place in the oven to heat through for 15 minutes.

◆ **VEGAN** ◆

Stir-fried Pak Choy

4 small pak choy

1 tbsp sunflower oil

1 tbsp lemon juice

Wasabi and Sesame Noodles

Japanese soba noodles, enough for 4

1 tsp wasabi paste

1 tbsp toasted sesame oil

2 tbsps sesame seeds, toasted

handful fresh coriander, chopped

Stir-fried Pak Choy

Slice the pak choy lengthways, each one into 4, and wash really well to remove the grit that gets caught between the leaves. Drain and then stir-fry quickly in the sunflower oil. When it's just cooked, which only takes a couple of minutes, add the lemon juice.

Wasabi and Sesame Noodles

Cook the soba noodles according to the instructions on the packet.

Mix the wasabi paste with the toasted sesame oil and toasted sesame seeds and toss into the hot noodles.

To serve

Heat up the remaining marinade and reduce to a syrupy consistency.

Serve by placing a swirl of Wasabi and Sesame Noodles on each plate, then arrange a scoop of Stir-fried Pak Choy in the centre and top with a round of Teriyaki Tofu. Spoon over the hot marinade and decorate with fresh coriander.

I remember the apple charlotte of my childhood — apples cooked to a purée with plenty of butter and sugar, all baked in a crisp brown bread mould. This savoury version is also in a bread mould, but with a light vegetable filling and a surprise nugget of goats' cheese.

Provençal Charlottes
with a Fresh Tomato and Basil Concassé

Pre-heat the oven to 200°C/Gas 6.

You will need 6 pudding moulds size 250 ml.

Charlotte Filling

Gently fry the spring onions, courgettes and celery in olive oil for a few minutes. Add the chilli and garlic and fry for another couple of minutes. Then add the tomatoes, passata, white wine, lemon juice, apple juice concentrate and the bunch of thyme. Simmer gently for 10 minutes, stirring occasionally. Take off the heat, add the parsley and basil and season to taste. Remove the bunch of thyme and leave to cool.

Next you need to line the pudding moulds with bread. You will need 4 to 5 slices of ciabatta for each mould. Mix the sun-dried tomato paste with the olive oil. Spread the oil-tomato mix on to one side of every slice of ciabatta.

With the slices oil side down, press the tip of the bread firmly to the base of the pudding mould so that it is sticking up lengthways against the inside. Repeat with another 4 or 5 slices until the mould is lined on the bottom and sides. It should look like the segments of an orange, with a couple of centimetres of bread sticking out of the top for folding over the filling. Repeat this step for all 6 moulds.

In the bottom of each lined mould, put a couple of cubes of goats' cheese, cover with the vegetable mixture and fill to the top. Then fold in the flaps of bread over the top, to seal the charlottes.

SERVES: 6

1 loaf ciabatta bread, cut into 1/2 cm thick slices

1 tbsp sun-dried tomato paste

10 tbsps olive oil

100 g goats' cheese, cut into 12 cubes

fresh chives for decoration, chopped

Charlotte Filling

1 tbsp olive oil

3 spring onions, chopped

200 g courgettes, diced small

150 g celery, chopped small

1/2 red chilli, finely chopped

4 garlic cloves, finely chopped

2 tomatoes, cored and diced

200 ml passata

50 ml white wine

1 tbsp lemon juice

1 tbsp apple juice concentrate

bunch of thyme, tied with string

2 tbsps fresh parsley, chopped

2 tbsps basil, chopped

salt and freshly ground black pepper

Passata is made from thick puréed tomatoes. Ideal for soups and sauces when you want a smooth texture. You can buy passata in cartons or jars. After opening keep in the fridge and use up in a few days.

Tomato and Basil Concassé

6 tomatoes, peeled and cored

2 tbsps olive oil

2 garlic cloves, finely chopped

1 tsp apple juice concentrate

handful of fresh basil, roughly chopped

salt and freshly ground black pepper

Metal pudding moulds come in various sizes and are also useful for individual steamed puddings, particularly Christmas puddings.
If you don't want to make individual charlottes, fill a large charlotte mould and just lengthen the cooking time.

Place a heavy weight on top of each charlotte to ensure that they are well and truly sealed. Then place them on a baking tray and bake in the pre-heated oven for 15 to 20 minutes, until the tops are crisp and golden.

Tomato and Basil Concassé

To peel tomatoes, make a slit in each one, put in a bowl, cover with boiling water and leave. After 5 minutes the skins should peel off easily.

Cut the tomatoes in half, core and roughly chop.

Heat the olive oil in a heavy-bottomed saucepan, add the garlic and sauté until just beginning to colour. Add the tomatoes, stir and simmer for a few minutes. The aim is to keep the tomatoes chunky, rather than create a smooth sauce.

Add the apple juice concentrate and fresh basil and then season with salt and freshly ground black pepper.

To serve

Leave the cooked charlottes to cool a little and then, with a small sharp knife, ease around the inside edge of each pudding mould so that the pudding slips out easily.

Turn the charlottes out onto warm plates, pour a little tomato and basil concassé around each charlotte and decorate with fresh chopped chives. Serve with seasonal vegetables and new potatoes.

This is a very warming winter dish. The portobello mushrooms are baked in a marinade flavoured with wine, brandy and herbs and served on a cashew crust, with baked tomatoes adding colour and contrast.

Brandied Portobello Mushrooms on a Tomato Cashew Crust

Pre-heat the oven to 180°C/Gas 5. Line a baking tray with baking parchment and grease 6 × 8 cm muffin rings.

For the crust

Blend all the ingredients together in a food processor. Place the muffin rings on the baking tray, divide the mixture between them and press down lightly. Bake in the pre-heated oven for 20 minutes or until golden. Leave to cool a little and then slip the rings off.

For the mushrooms

Slice off the stalks and place the mushrooms in an oiled baking dish just big enough for them to fit in tightly. Sprinkle with slices of garlic, rosemary and thyme. Make up the marinade and pour over the mushrooms. Bake in the pre-heated oven for 30 minutes. Remove the mushrooms from the marinade and set aside. Strain the marinade into a saucepan and reduce to a thick sauce.

For the tomatoes

To cook the tomatoes place the slices on a baking tray, drizzle with olive oil and bake for 10 minutes in the pre-heated oven.

To reheat, place the crusts on a baking tray, top with two slices of tomatoes and then one or two mushrooms, depending on size, each mushroom cut into quarters and fanned out on top of the tomatoes. Drizzle with a drop of olive oil and a good twist of black pepper and reheat for 10 minutes. Heat up the sauce.

To serve

Place a mushroom topped crust on each plate and spoon on the sauce. Serve with steamed broccoli, spinach or curly kale.

SERVES 6

For the crust

100 g cashew nuts, ground

100 g ground almonds

100 g white breadcrumbs

4 garlic cloves, crushed

100 g margarine

pinch of salt

For the mushrooms

6 large portobello mushrooms or 12 medium

1 tbsp olive oil

6 garlic cloves, thinly sliced

1 tbsp fresh rosemary

1 tbsp fresh thyme

For the marinade

200 ml white wine

100 ml brandy

100 ml water

3 tbsps shoyu

1 tbsp apple juice concentrate

For the tomatoes

3 tomatoes, each cut into 4 slices

1 tbsp olive oil

♦ **VEGAN** ♦

Polenta was, traditionally, as much the staple carbohydrate of northern Italy as pasta was to the south. It is made from fine yellow cornmeal and can be enriched with butter, olive oil, cheese or herbs. Its consistency varies from soft, like mashed potato, to firm for grilling.

Smoky Polenta
with Artichoke, Olive and Caper Sauce

In a large saucepan bring the water to the boil and add the salt and olive oil. Remove from the heat and slowly pour in the polenta, stirring with a wooden spoon or whisk.

Return the saucepan to the heat and keep stirring until the polenta is thick and smooth. It is cooked when it falls away from the sides of the saucepan and is no longer granular in texture. Add the grated smoked cheese and stir in.

Pour the cooked polenta into an oiled 30 cm ceramic dish or tart tin, smooth over and leave until completely cold and solid.

Artichoke, Olive and Caper Sauce

Pre-heat the oven to 220°C/Gas 7.

Put the sliced peppers and the quartered tomatoes on a baking tray with 2 tablespoons of olive oil and roast in the pre-heated oven for 15–20 minutes.

In a saucepan fry the onions in the remaining olive oil until soft. Add the garlic and fry for a few more minutes. Add the roasted peppers and tomatoes to the onion mix and cook for 10 minutes.

Stir in the artichoke hearts, capers, olives, red wine, red grape juice and apple juice concentrate and simmer gently for a further 30 minutes. Season with salt and plenty of freshly ground black pepper and finally add the fresh herbs.

To serve

To serve, cut the polenta into triangular wedges, brush with olive oil and place under a hot grill until golden. Arrange the grilled polenta on a serving dish or on individual plates and spoon over the hot sauce. Serve with a green leaf and fresh herb salad.

SERVES 4/6

250 g polenta, 'easy cook'

1 litre water

1 level tsp salt

1 tbsp olive oil

200 g smoked cheese, grated

Artichoke, Olive and Caper Sauce

2 red peppers, sliced

6 tomatoes, quartered

3 tbsps olive oil

1 medium red onion, chopped

4 garlic cloves, peeled and finely chopped

1 tin of artichoke hearts, drained and halved

100 g black olives, pitted and halved

50 g capers, drained

100 ml organic red wine

100 ml red grape juice

1 tbsp apple juice concentrate

salt and plenty of freshly ground black pepper

a handful of fresh herbs, chopped

One of my favourite autumnal dishes, it combines fresh butternut squash with a smoked Cheddar cheese and is served with a tangy lemon sauce to cut through the richness of the rissoles.

Butternut Squash and Cheddar Rissoles
with a Lemon and Chive Sauce

SERVES 4/6

450 g butternut squash

45 ml olive oil

60 g wild rice

250 ml water

1 tsp vegetable bouillon powder

½ red onion, peeled and finely chopped

2 garlic cloves, finely chopped

1 small carrot, peeled and diced small

60 g risotto rice

1 tbsp fresh oregano, finely chopped

1 tbsp fresh thyme, finely chopped

1 tsp paprika

75 g smoked Cheddar, grated

1 tbsp lemon juice

a dash of Tabasco

salt and freshly ground black pepper

50 g polenta for rolling the rissoles in

sunflower oil for frying

Pre-heat the oven to 220°C/Gas 7.

Prepare the squash by peeling off the skin with either a potato peeler or small sharp knife. Cut the squash in half lengthways. Scoop out the seeds and cut into 1 cm cubes.

Heat 2 tablespoons of olive oil in a roasting tin. Add the cubed squash and roast in the pre-heated oven for 30 minutes.

Cook the wild rice in plenty of water for 45 minutes or until tender. You can tell it is cooked when the seeds pop out of their shiny black sheaths. Undercooked rice will explode when the rissoles are fried and completely ruin the dish. You have been warned!

Make up a vegetable stock with 1 teaspoon vegetable bouillon powder to 250 ml boiling water.

Reserve half the roasted squash and purée the rest with 75 ml of stock.

Heat the rest of the olive oil in a large saucepan and gently fry the red onion, garlic and carrots, until the carrots are just cooked.

Add the risotto rice and stir-fry for 2 minutes. Then over a low heat, add the hot stock a little at a time, letting the rice absorb the liquid before adding more, stirring to stop the rice from sticking.

When the rice has absorbed all the stock, add the squash purée and cook for 2-3 minutes.

Add the roasted squash cubes, cooked wild rice, herbs, paprika, smoked cheese, lemon juice and Tabasco. Mix well and season with salt and pepper. Leave the mix to cool.

Shape into 5 cm x 2 cm high rissoles and roll in polenta.

In a large non-stick frying pan, add a little sunflower oil and fry the rissoles on a medium heat until crisp and golden on both sides.

Lemon and Chive Sauce

Put the lemon juice and zest, apple juice concentrate and sugar in a saucepan and simmer until the sugar has dissolved.

Dissolve the vegetable bouillon powder in the boiling water. Add to the lemon sauce and simmer for 5 minutes. Add the chopped chives and take the sauce off the heat.

To serve

Serve two rissoles per person with the Lemon and Chive Sauce and steamed seasonal vegetables.

Lemon and Chive Sauce

1 organic unwaxed lemon, zest and juice

1 tbsp apple juice concentrate

50 g caster sugar

150 ml boiling water

1 tsp vegetable bouillon powder

2 tbsps chives, finely chopped

The cardamom in these soufflé cakes gives them a subtle Eastern flavour. They are easy to make and look great on the plate with a striking colour combination of the orange from the carrots, green from the spinach and red from the sauce.

Carrot and Cardamom Soufflé Cakes
with Fresh Spinach and a Red Pepper Sauce

SERVES 6

350 g carrots, peeled and chopped

200 g Greek yoghurt

6 eggs, separated

50 g Cheddar, grated

6 cardamom pods, shelled and seeds crushed

salt and freshly ground black pepper

olive oil for frying

500 g fresh spinach

Pre-heat the oven to 190°C/Gas 5.

You will need 6 x 10 cm scone/muffin rings.

Cook the carrots until just tender, but not mushy. Drain very well and leave to cool.

To get at the cardamom seeds, dry roast the cardamom pods until they begin to split, take off the heat and split open. Shake the little black seeds into a mortar and grind with a pestle to a powder.

When the carrots are cool, roughly mash them and add the yoghurt, beaten egg yolks, cheese, cardamom powder and seasoning. Mix well.

In a separate bowl whisk the egg whites into soft peaks. Then with a large metal spoon fold the beaten egg whites into the carrot mixture.

Oil the insides of the scone rings. Line a baking tray with parchment and place the oiled scone rings on the tray. Spoon the carrot mix into the rings till 3/4 full.

Bake in the middle of the pre-heated oven for 20 minutes until the soufflés have puffed up and are golden on top. Check they are cooked through by piercing with a skewer. If the skewer comes out clean they are cooked through.

Let the soufflé cakes cool for 5 minutes and then, with a small sharp knife, run round the inside of each scone ring and very gently remove them.

Steam the spinach and drain thoroughly.

Red Pepper Sauce

3 red peppers, halved and deseeded

1 tbsp olive oil

1 small onion, chopped

3 garlic cloves, chopped

50 ml white wine

400 g tin plum tomatoes, chopped

1 tbsp lemon juice

1 tsp apple juice concentrate

salt and freshly ground black pepper

Red Pepper Sauce

Place the pepper halves under a hot grill skin side up and grill until blistered and beginning to char. To make the peeling easy, place them in a bowl. Cover the top of the bowl tightly with cling film and leave the peppers for 20 minutes to sweat and cool. Peel off the skins, roughly chop and set aside.

Fry the onion in the olive oil until soft. Add the garlic and wine and simmer for a few minutes, then add the chopped tomatoes and cook until the tomatoes have broken down.

Add the lemon juice and apple juice concentrate and season well. Leave to cool a little before liquidising.

Put the peppers and the tomato mixture into the liquidiser and purée to a smooth consistency. You may need to add a little water if it's too thick. Warm the sauce before serving.

To serve

To serve, put a circle of spinach, a little bigger than the soufflé cakes, on each plate, place a hot soufflé cake in the centre of each spinach circle and drizzle the Red Pepper Sauce around the spinach.

*This is a very simple dish and great for impromptu dinner parties.
The individual pastry boxes look impressive on the plate, with
the cherry tomatoes and red peppers contrasting
with the green sauce.*

Tomato and Pepper Puff Pastry Boxes
with *Spinach Sauce*

Pre-heat the oven to 180°C/Gas 4.

Roll out the pastry to 1/2 cm thick and divide into 10 cm squares. Lightly score an inner square on each pastry square, leaving a 1.5 cm border.

Brush the inner square with pesto and top with the tomatoes, pepper cubes and pinenuts, leaving the border bare. Brush the border with milk or soya milk.

Place the squares on an oiled tray and bake in the pre-heated oven for 20-25 minutes until puffed up and golden, and serve at once.

Spinach Sauce

Cook the spinach in a little water until wilted, drain and leave to cool in cold water so that it retains its green colour. When cold squeeze out all the water and set aside.

Sauté the garlic in the butter, add the flour and stir with a wooden spoon until the butter and flour form a paste. Slowly add the milk, stirring all the time. Then add the mustard and bouillon and stir until the sauce has thickened.

Chop the spinach finely and add to the sauce. For a smooth green sauce whiz with a hand blender or in a liquidiser. Check for seasoning.

To serve

Serve the pastry boxes hot in a puddle of green Spinach Sauce.

SERVES 4

340 g packet puff pastry

250 g cherry tomatoes, halved

1 red pepper, cut in small chunks

50 g pinenuts

2 tbsps pesto

Spinach Sauce

125 g fresh or frozen spinach

25 g butter or margarine

1 garlic clove, crushed

25 g white flour

500 ml milk or soya milk

1 tsp mustard

1/2 tsp vegetable bouillon powder

salt and freshly ground black pepper

Buy frozen puff pastry and unfreeze a couple of hours before you need it.

♦ VEGAN ♦

Christmas time at Demuths is never complete without this traditional roast which we serve with all the trimmings and roasted organic potatoes.

Christmas Roast
with Mushroom Gravy and Cranberry Relish

SERVES 6

100 g green lentils

2 bay leaves

500 ml stock made with 1 tsp vegetable bouillon powder

2 tbsps sunflower oil

1 large red onion, finely sliced

2 garlic cloves, finely chopped

1/2 tsp turmeric powder

1/2 tsp chilli powder

1/2 tsp ginger powder

2 carrots, grated (200 g)

2 courgettes, grated (200 g)

100 g medium oatmeal

100 g chopped cashews

50 g sunflower seeds, toasted

50 g pumpkin seeds, toasted

50 g sesame seeds, toasted

2 tbsps tamari

1 tbsp tomato purée

1 tbsp fresh parsley, chopped

salt and freshly ground black pepper

Pre-heat the oven to 180°C/Gas 4.

Wash the green lentils, put them in a small saucepan with the stock and bay leaves. Bring to the boil and simmer until the lentils are tender, drain, remove the bay leaves and set aside.

Mix all the seeds together on a baking sheet and place under the grill on the lowest rung (i.e. as far away from the heat as possible). Toast them until they just begin to tan, stir them and toast again, being very careful not to let them burn, as this will ruin the flavour of the roast.

Fry the onion in the sunflower oil until translucent, add the garlic and spices and stir-fry quickly. Add the carrots and courgettes and stir-fry for 5 minutes.

Now add the cooked lentils, oatmeal, cashews, two thirds of the toasted seeds, the tamari, tomato purée and parsley. Season with salt and freshly ground black pepper.

Grease a large loaf tin and line with baking parchment, sprinkle the remaining seeds into the tin and then spoon on the roast mixture. Press the mixture down into the tin, cover the top with baking parchment and bake in the middle of the pre-heated oven for 45 minutes or until firm. Remove the baking parchment from the top and bake for a further 10 minutes.

Leave to cool in the tin for 10 minutes before turning out on to a serving dish.

Porcini and Oyster Mushroom Gravy

Rehydrate the dried porcini mushrooms by covering with boiling water and leaving for 30 minutes.

Fry the onion in the olive oil until just beginning to turn brown. Add the garlic and quickly stir-fry. Add the red wine, red grape juice, apple juice concentrate, stock and rosemary and simmer gently for about 30 minutes or until reduced by a third.

Fry the oyster mushrooms in the olive oil, tamari and plenty of black pepper. Add the cooked oyster mushrooms, the re-hydrated porcini mushrooms plus the soaking liquid to the gravy. Strain the soaking liquid through a tea strainer, as dried mushrooms are often gritty.

Mix the cornflour with a little cold water to a smooth paste and add this to the gravy. Simmer gently until reduced to the desired consistency. Remove the rosemary sprig before serving and season to taste.

Cranberry Relish

Place the cranberries in a saucepan and cover with water, but not enough to allow the berries to float.

Peel the lemon with a potato peeler. Add the spices and lemon peel to the cranberries and bring to the boil. Simmer slowly until about half the berries have popped. Stir in the sugar and lemon juice. Simmer on a low heat, stirring often, until all the sugar has dissolved. Serve cold.

To serve

To serve, cut the roast into thick slices with a sharp serrated knife and serve with the Mushroom Gravy, a spoonful of Cranberry Relish and roasted organic potatoes.

Porcini and Oyster Mushroom Gravy

10 g dried porcini mushrooms

1 small onion, finely sliced

1 tbsp olive oil

2 garlic cloves, crushed

150 ml vegan red wine

75 ml red grape juice

1 tsp apple juice concentrate

1 tsp vegetable bouillon powder mixed with 500 ml boiling water

a sprig of rosemary

100 g oyster mushrooms

1 tbsp olive oil

1 tbsp tamari

1 tsp cornflour

salt and freshly ground black pepper

Cranberry Relish

225 g fresh cranberries

4 cardamom pods

1/2 cinnamon stick

2 cloves

2 star anise

100 g caster sugar

1 lemon, peel and 1/2 the juice

◆ VEGAN ◆

These beef tomatoes are stuffed with a fiery hot tofu, sweetcorn and pepper filling and are best served with a cooling herb and yoghurt raita.

Cajun Beefy Tomatoes

SERVES 6

6 beef tomatoes

285 g plain tofu
1 tsp olive oil
1 tsp paprika

1 red onion, finely chopped
1 tbsp olive oil
6 garlic cloves, finely chopped
1 red chilli, finely sliced

100 g sweetcorn kernels
1 green pepper, diced
1 tsp apple juice concentrate
1 tsp lemon juice
1 tsp wine vinegar
2 tbsps fresh coriander, chopped

Cajun Spice Mix
2 tsps paprika
1 tsp ground ginger
1 tsp ground cumin
$1/2$ tsp cayenne
$1/2$ tsp ground fennel
$1/2$ tsp salt
freshly ground black pepper

Pre-heat the oven to 225°C/Gas 7.

Cut the tops off the tomatoes about 1cm from the crown and set aside. Scoop out the insides to about $1/2$ cm all round and set the outers aside. Then roughly chop the scooped out tomato inners, discarding any pithy bits.

Drain the tofu and cut into 1 cm cubes, toss in olive oil, sprinkle with paprika and roast in the pre-heated oven for 25 minutes or until crisp.

Cajun Spice Mix

Make up the Cajun Spice Mix by combining all the ingredients in a bowl.

Fry the onion in the olive oil until translucent, add the garlic and chilli and fry for a couple more minutes. Add the spice mix and stir-fry until fragrant. Add the chopped tomato inners and simmer until almost all the liquid has evaporated. Then add the sweetcorn and green pepper and simmer until the green pepper is soft.

Take off the heat and add the apple juice concentrate, lemon juice and wine vinegar. Finally, stir in the roasted tofu and the chopped coriander.

Stuff the tomato outers with the filling, put their top hats back on and bake for 15 minutes.

To serve

Serve with a cooling herb and yoghurt raita (see page 188), plain basmati rice and a green salad.

A delicious Burgundy wine-rich casserole that can be made a few days in advance and served as an alternative Christmas Day dish.

Bourguignonne of Chestnuts, Mushrooms and Roasted Garlic

Pre-heat the oven to 200°C/Gas 6.

Use a large, deep baking tray, big enough to take all the vegetables, otherwise use two and split the vegetables between them.

Heat the olive oil in the baking tray. Add the garlic cloves and halved shallots and roast for 15 minutes.

Add the celeriac, celery and red peppers, stir well and roast for another 30 minutes. At this point decant the vegetables into a large ovenproof casserole dish with a lid.

Stir in the cooked chestnuts, mushrooms and herbs and season with a pinch of salt and plenty of freshly ground black pepper. Add the wine, tamari, tomato purée and stock.

Either reduce the heat in the oven to 150°C/Gas 2 and cook for a further 2 hours or simmer gently on the top for 1 hour. Stir occasionally to prevent the vegetables sticking and add more water if necessary.

Thicken the sauce with the cornflour paste and check for seasoning.

To serve

Serve with all the Christmas trimmings or with a pile of creamy mashed potato.

SERVES 4/6

250 g cooked whole chestnuts

50 ml olive oil

1 bulb garlic, peeled and the cloves left whole

400 g shallots, peeled and halved

½ small celeriac, peeled and cubed

2 sticks celery, washed and chopped

2 red peppers, sliced

250 g button mushrooms

2 bay leaves

1 tbsp fresh chopped rosemary

1 tbsp fresh chopped thyme

salt and freshly ground black pepper

300 ml vegan red wine

1 tbsp tamari

1 tbsp tomato purée

500 ml stock made with 1 tsp vegetable bouillon powder

½ tsp cornflour, mixed to a paste with cold water

Celeriac is a knobbly root with a thick skin, available from local greengrocers and most supermarkets. It's related to celery, but with a subtle flavour. Delicious in soups, mashed with potatoes or grated raw for a winter salad. If eaten raw celeriac must be mixed with lemon juice, as it discolours.

♦ VEGAN ♦

Chilli Meals

It's amazing how we associate India and South East Asia with hot and spicy food, when the reality is that the humble chilli is native only to Central and South America. They have been cultivated there since 3500 BC and were only introduced to India by the colonial Portuguese in the 16th century. As the people of India and South East Asia were accustomed to eating food made hot from black pepper, they enthusiastically adopted the chilli as their own.

The heat of the chilli comes from the alkaloid 'capsaicin', which is particularly prominent in the white membrane that holds the seeds in the chilli. The seeds are the next hottest, so for a milder flavour scrape out the membrane and then if necessary the seeds.

There are more than 200 different types of chilli, generally the smaller the size, the more powerful the heat. Red chillies are not necessarily hotter than green, as red chillies are ripe and tend to be sweeter. Chillies are rich in vitamin C and also trigger your endorphins and hence can become addictive.

Be very careful preparing chillies as there is nothing worse than chilli oil in the eyes, so wash your hands really well with soapy water before touching any sensitive parts of your body.

Laksa Lemak is a Malay coconut and noodle soup from Malacca. A meal in itself, it's very rich and spicy and best served in deep Chinese bowls with chopsticks and a spoon to slurp up the coconut gravy.

Laksa Lemak

SERVES 4

1 tbsp sunflower oil

2 large shallots, finely chopped

1 red pepper, thinly sliced

1 tin coconut milk (400 ml)

750 ml boiling water

2 lime leaves

2 pak choy, thinly sliced

1 tbsp tamari

1 tsp sugar

1/2 lime, juiced

1/2 tsp turmeric

1/2 tsp salt

285 g plain tofu

handful of beansprouts

4 spring onions, sliced into rings

1 red chilli, finely sliced

fresh coriander, chopped

200 g dried rice vermicelli

Spice Paste

thumb sized piece of ginger root, peeled and chopped

2 garlic cloves, peeled and chopped

1 red chilli, deseeded and thinly sliced

1 stalk lemongrass, finely chopped

Firstly you will need to make up the Spice Paste.

Spice Paste

Whiz the ginger, garlic, chilli and lemon grass to a smooth paste in a mini food processor. Alternatively you can pummel them to a paste using a pestle and mortar. Either way, add a little oil to ease the process.

Heat a large heavy-bottomed saucepan, add the oil and fry the shallots until golden. Add the spice paste, turmeric and salt and stir-fry until fragrant, taking care that the spices don't burn. Add the red pepper and stir-fry for a couple of minutes.

Pour in the coconut milk, water and lime leaves. Bring to the boil, turn down the heat and simmer gently, uncovered, for 10 minutes.

Add the pak choy, tamari and sugar and simmer for a few minutes, finally adding the lime juice and season to taste.

While the soup is cooking, prepare the garnish ingredients. Slice the tofu into matchstick size pieces and fry these in sunflower oil until golden. Drain on kitchen paper. Rinse the beansprouts, slice the spring onions and red chilli and chop the coriander.

To serve

Soak the rice vermicelli in warm water for 3–5 minutes. Drain and divide between 4 deep Chinese bowls. Add the beansprouts and pour on the hot soup. Garnish with tofu matchsticks, spring onions, red chilli and coriander.

This Saag Paneer is chunky with the fresh spinach cut coarse and the Indian cheese crisp and golden. Delicious served with red rice and sweet date chutney.

Saag Paneer
with Red Rice and Iranganis' Date Pickle

SERVES 4

250 g paneer, cubed

3 tbsps sunflower oil

1 onion, chopped

2 garlic cloves, finely chopped

thumb of ginger, peeled and finely chopped

2 green chillies, finely chopped

1/2 tsp turmeric

1/2 tsp chilli

1 tsp cumin

1 tsp salt

2 tomatoes, chopped

500 g spinach, washed and roughly chopped

1 tbsp lemon juice

salt and freshly ground black pepper

Red rice, enough for 4

In a wok or large saucepan fry the onion in 2 tablespoons of sunflower oil until golden. Add the garlic and stir-fry for a minute, then add the ginger, chillies, spices and salt, stir-fry until fragrant.

Add the tomatoes and stir-fry for a minute. Then add the spinach and lemon juice, mix well, turn down the heat, cover with a lid and cook until the spinach is tender.

In a separate frying pan fry the paneer in the remaining oil, turning the cubes over so that they cook on all sides, until golden.

Add the paneer to the spinach, stir in and gently simmer for 5 minutes. Season with salt and freshly ground black pepper.

Cook the red rice according to the instructions on the packet.

To serve

Serve the Saag Paneer with a pile of red rice and Iranganis' Date Pickle (see page 185).

Saag is a general Indian term for green vegetables. Methi (fenugreek leaves) are often used but are difficult to get here, so spinach or chard is the best alternative.

Indian red rice is hard to buy over here, as it's not considered a high enough quality for export. As a substitute use French Camargue red rice, which has a lovely nutty flavour.

The highlands of Ethiopia, when not in the throes of drought or war, can grow a vast range of vegetables and fruit. The Coptic Christians, who live in this region, have a long tradition of vegetarian cooking as they abstain from eating meat for two hundred days each year.

Yetakelt W'et
A Spicy Ethiopian Vegetable Stew with a Fruit and Nut Pilaf

An Ethiopian meal always has as its basis a w'et (stew) flavoured with berbere, a carefully balanced mix of spices unique to Ethiopia. This is eaten with a flat bread made with t'eff, a type of millet.

You will first need to make the niter kebbeh, a spiced clarified butter which is used to fry the vegetables for the w'et, and the berbere Ethiopian hot spice mixture.

Niter Kebbeh Spiced Clarified Butter

Heat the vegetable ghee in a saucepan, add all the other ingredients and simmer very gently for 30 minutes. Strain the ghee and discard the spices.

Store any unused niter kebbeh in a sealed container in the fridge, it will keep for a couple of months. Niter kebbeh is also great as a basis for Indian curries.

SERVES 4/6

Niter Kebbeh Spiced Clarified Butter

250 ml vegetable ghee

1 shallot, chopped

2 garlic cloves, crushed

1 tbsp fresh ginger root, peeled and diced

1/4 tsp turmeric

2 cardamom seeds, crushed

1/2 cinnamon stick

1/4 tsp ground fenugreek

Berbere Ethiopian Hot Spice Mixture

1 tsp cumin seeds

1/2 tsp cardamom seeds

1/2 tsp fenugreek seeds

1/2 tsp coriander seeds

2 whole cloves

1/4 tsp black peppercorns

1/4 tsp whole allspice

1 tsp dried chilli flakes

1/2 tsp ginger powder

1/4 tsp turmeric

1/4 tsp cinnamon

1/2 tsp salt

1 tbsp paprika

♦ VEGAN ♦

Yetakelt W'et

1 onion, peeled and chopped

3 tbsps niter kebbeh

2 garlic cloves, peeled and crushed

1 tbsp berbere

1 tbsp paprika

2 carrots, peeled and chopped

1 potato, peeled and cubed

1 sweet potato, peeled and cubed

1/4 squash, peeled and cubed

4 tomatoes, chopped

1 tbsp tomato paste

vegetable stock to cover

100 g green beans, topped and tailed and cut into thirds.

250 g spinach, washed and destalked

salt and freshly ground black pepper

Fruit and Nut Pilaf

350 g long grain brown rice

4 tbsps olive oil

1 onion, finely chopped

750 ml vegetable stock

1 tbsp olive oil

1/2 tsp ground cinnamon

1/4 tsp ground nutmeg

50 g dried apricots, soaked and chopped

50 g dates, soaked and chopped

25 g flaked almonds, toasted

2 tbsps orange juice

1 tbsp tamari

Berbere Ethiopian Hot Spice Mixture

Dry-fry the seeds, cloves, peppercorns and allspice until fragrant, cool and then grind in a spice grinder or pestle and mortar along with the chilli flakes. Mix in the other ingredients. Store unused berbere in a sealed container.

Yetakelt W'et

Fry the onion in the niter kebbeh until translucent. Add the garlic, berbere and paprika and fry gently for a couple of minutes. Add the carrots, potato, sweet potato and squash. Fry gently for 10 minutes, stirring occasionally to stop the vegetables from burning.

Add the chopped tomatoes, tomato paste and vegetable stock. Bring to the boil and simmer for 10 minutes.

Blanch the green beans separately and add these together with the spinach. Simmer for a further 5 minutes and season to taste.

Fruit and Nut Pilaf

Soak the rice in cold water for 30 minutes, and drain.

Heat the olive oil, add the onion and fry until golden. Add the rice, lower the heat and stir-fry for 5 minutes. Add the vegetable stock, cover and cook until the rice is tender and the stock has been absorbed.

In a separate saucepan heat the remaining olive oil, add the spices, apricots, dates and almonds and fry for a few minutes. Add the orange juice and tamari and set aside. Stir the fruit and nut mixture into the rice.

To serve

On a large plate serve the Fruit and Nut Pilaf with a generous helping of Yetakelt W'et on top and warm pitta bread to mop up the juices.

Vietnamese Buddhists traditionally refrain from eating garlic, onions and chillies. In this recipe though, I have included them to liven things up. Quick and easy to make.

Vietnamese Pumpkin and Coconut Curry

Firstly you will need to make up the garlic paste. Whiz the garlic, chilli and ginger in a mini food processor; alternatively use a pestle and mortar.

Heat the sunflower oil in a large heavy-bottomed saucepan, add the onion and stir-fry until golden. Then add the garlic paste and stir-fry until fragrant. Add the spices and stir-fry for 1 minute.

Add the coconut milk and water, stir well and bring to the boil. Turn down the heat and simmer for 5 minutes.

Add the pumpkin and sweet potato and simmer for 15 minutes, then add the courgette and simmer until tender.

Add the lime juice and fresh coriander and taste for seasoning.

To serve

Serve with Thai fragrant rice.

SERVES 4

Garlic Paste

4 garlic cloves, chopped

1 red chilli, chopped

2.5 cm fresh ginger, peeled and chopped

1 tbsp sunflower oil

1 onion, sliced

1 tsp turmeric

8 cardamom pods, crushed

small piece cinnamon bark

400 ml coconut milk

150 ml water

250 g pumpkin, peeled and cut into cubes

125 g sweet potato, peeled and cut into cubes

125 g courgette, cut into cubes

1 tbsp lime juice

handful of fresh chopped coriander

salt and pepper

The origins of Gumbo come from the African plant hibiscus — okra or ladies fingers. Called by its Angolan name Ochinggombo it was taken to America with the slaves and gave its name to this hot fiery stew.

Gumbo Ya Ya
with Yellow Corn Bread

SERVES 4/6

2 tbsps olive oil

1 onion, diced small

1 small leek, cut in 1cm thick half moons

6 garlic cloves, peeled and finely chopped

3 hot red chillies, deseeded and finely sliced

1 tsp paprika

1 small red pepper, sliced in 1cm wide fingers

1 small green pepper, sliced in 1 cm wide fingers

2 sticks celery, washed and sliced

300 ml passata

100 ml water

1 medium sized sweet potato, peeled and cut in 3 cm chunks

50 g sun-dried tomatoes, halved

100 g fresh okra, washed, topped, tailed and cut into thirds

3 tbsps fresh thyme, de-stemmed

salt and freshly ground black pepper

Fry the onions in olive oil until soft and translucent. Stir in the sliced leeks and fry for a few minutes before adding the garlic, chilli and paprika.

Add the peppers and celery and stir-fry, then add the passata and water and bring to the boil.

Turn down to a simmer, add the sweet potato and sun-dried tomatoes and simmer for 15 minutes until the sweet potato is just tender. You may need to add a little more water if the Gumbo gets too thick.

Finally, add the okra and fresh thyme and season with salt and freshly ground black pepper. Simmer gently for 10 minutes.

Okra is the seed-pod of the hibiscus esculentus and is also known as ladies fingers, bindi and gumbo. They are bright green, ridged and about the size of a finger. When cut they exude a gelatinous, slimy and viscous goo from their mucilaginous seeds. For Gumbo, this is the key ingredient, thickening the stew and giving it its shiny, jelly-like quality.

♦ VEGAN ♦

Yellow Cornbread

200 g fine yellow cornmeal

50 g brown rice flour

4 tsps baking powder

1 tbsp caster sugar

1 heaped tsp paprika

1/2 tsp salt

75 ml sunflower oil

25 ml olive oil

1 tbsp sunflower margarine, melted

200 ml water

100 ml soya cream

80 ml apple juice

Yellow Cornbread

Pre-heat the oven to 200°C/Gas 6.

Grease and line a 450 g loaf tin with baking parchment.

Mix all the dry ingredients together in a large bowl. Then mix all the wet ingredients together and add these to the dry ones. Mix to a smooth batter.

Pour this batter into the prepared loaf tin and bake in the middle of the pre-heated oven until golden – about 45 minutes. Test that it is cooked with a skewer. If the skewer comes out dry, the cornbread is cooked through.

Leave to cool before cutting.

To serve

Serve the Gumbo in a bowl with large slices of cornbread and a green leaf salad.

Creole cooking was imported into the southern states of the USA during the 18th century by French settlers. Based on rice, beans and tomatoes, this dish is flavoured with a distinctive Cajun spice mix.

Creole Rice and Beans
with Avocado and Kiwi Salsa

Cook the rice and set aside.

Fry the onion in the olive oil until soft and translucent. Add the garlic, chilli and Cajun spice mix and stir-fry until fragrant. Then add the peppers and stir-fry for a few minutes more.

Drain and rinse the beans and add these, together with the tomatoes, passata, apple juice concentrate, lemon juice and herbs and cook gently for 10 minutes. Stir in the cooked rice, heat through, and season to taste.

Avocado and Kiwi Salsa

Peel the avocado and kiwi fruit and cut both into small cubes. Then mix all the ingredients together and serve at once, as the avocado will discolour.

To serve

Serve the Rice and Beans together with a green leaf salad and accompanied by the Avocado and Kiwi Salsa.

I have suggested using a ready made Cajun spice mix in this recipe. If you want to make your own you will need 1 tsp paprika, 1/2 tsp cayenne, 1/2 tsp cumin, 1/2 tsp ground ginger, 1/4 tsp ground fennel, 1/2 tsp salt and a twist of black pepper. This will make more than enough for this recipe, the excess should be kept in an airtight container.

SERVES 4

150 g organic long grain brown rice

1 tbsp olive oil

1 onion, peeled and finely chopped

2 garlic cloves, peeled and finely chopped

1 red chilli, finely chopped

1 tsp Cajun spice mix

1 green pepper, chopped

1 red pepper, chopped

400 g tin mixed beans

3 tomatoes, diced

150 ml passata

1 tsp apple juice concentrate

1 tbsp lemon juice

1 tbsp fresh thyme

1 tbsp fresh basil, chopped

salt and freshly ground black pepper

Avocado and Kiwi Salsa

1 avocado

1 kiwi fruit

2 spring onions, finely sliced

1 tbsp fresh coriander, chopped

1/2 lime, juiced

1 tsp apple juice concentrate

♦ VEGAN ♦

Puri are Indian deep-fried chapatis which puff up when cooked. They are sometimes called poori and are sold all over India by street vendors.

Sweet Potato Puri
with *Spicy Indian Roast Vegetables and Cucumber Chutney*

SERVES 6

Spice Mix

1 tsp ground cumin

1 tsp ground coriander

1 tsp ground ginger

1 tsp turmeric

1 tsp cayenne

1 tsp fennel seeds

1 tsp garam masala

1 tsp salt

Spicy Indian Roast Vegetables

200 g organic new potatoes

1 small onion, sliced

6 garlic cloves, whole

7 tbsps vegetable ghee

1 small butternut squash, peeled and cut into chunks

1 courgette, thickly sliced

1 red pepper, in chunks

1 yellow pepper, in chunks

1 small cauliflower, florets only

100 g frozen organic peas

2 tomatoes, chopped large

handful of fresh coriander, chopped

Puri need to be eaten as soon as they are cooked, before they deflate, so make sure the Spicy Indian Roasted Vegetables and Cucumber Chutney are made first.

Spice Mix

The first step is to make the spice mix by simply combining all the ingredients.

Spicy Indian Roast Vegetables

Pre-heat the oven to 225°C/Gas 7.

This curry is chunky and takes time to cook, about 1 hour, depending on the size you have cut the vegetables.

Cut the new potatoes in half if small or quarter if larger. Par-boil until just beginning to soften.

Melt the ghee in a roasting pan large enough to hold all the vegetables. Add the onion, whole garlic cloves and the spices. Stir well and then add the potatoes and squash and roast for 15 minutes.

Add the courgette and peppers, stir again and roast for another 10 minutes. Then add the cauliflower and frozen peas, stir again and roast until the cauliflower is cooked – about 10 minutes.

Finally, add the chopped tomatoes and coriander, and return to the oven for a final 10 minutes.

We use a vegan ghee made from vegetable oil. Ghee is traditionally made from clarified unsalted butter, but it is not particularly healthy as it is high in cholesterol.

◆ VEGAN ◆

Cucumber Chutney

In a food processor, firstly purée the garlic and chilli, then add the green pepper and mint and whiz again. Finally, add the cucumber and whiz again, maintaining a chunky quality.

Stir in the apple juice concentrate, lime juice and salt.

Sweet Potato Puri

This mix makes 12 puri.

Cook the sweet potato, drain and mash.

In a large bowl mix all the ingredients together and knead the dough into a soft ball, if too sticky add a little more wholemeal flour. Knead for 5 minutes until the dough is elastic. Cover and set aside for 30 minutes.

On a well-floured surface, divide the dough into 12 equal portions and roll each one out thinly into 2 mm thick, roughly round shapes.

In a wok or large saucepan deep-fry the puri in sunflower oil one or two at a time. Watch them puff up and then carefully flip them over for a few seconds. Check the first one to make sure that it is cooked through. If it's still doughy in the middle roll the other puri out a little thinner, before frying. Eat the puri as quickly as possible before they deflate.

To serve

Serve the spicy vegetables with hot puri and the cucumber chutney on the side.

Cucumber Chutney

3 garlic cloves, chopped

1 green chilli, chopped

1/2 green pepper, chopped

2 tbsps fresh mint, chopped

1/2 cucumber, roughly chopped

1 tsp apple juice concentrate

1 lime, juiced

pinch of salt

Sweet Potato Puri

200 g sweet potato, peeled

50 g wholewheat flour

100 g plain white flour

pinch of salt

1 tsp ground cinnamon

25 ml olive oil

1 tbsp pomegranate seeds or finely chopped dried apricot

sunflower oil for deep-frying

Pomegranate seeds, also known as anardana seeds, are from the sour pomegranate. They are dried, have a lovely ruby colour and a sweet and sour flavour. Available from Indian stores.

Thali are the most popular lunchtime dish eaten in south India. They take their name from the metal plates they are served in. These contain three to six smaller katori (bowls) or indents in the plate, in each of which a different dish is served.

Southern Indian Thali
with Green Vegetable and Potato Mallung

SERVES 6

Paneer Tawa Masala, spicy fried paneer

250 g paneer, cubed

50 g butter ghee

1/2 tsp ajowan seeds

1 small onion, chopped

a thumb sized piece of ginger root, peeled and chopped

2 green chillies, deseeded and chopped

1/2 tsp chilli powder

1/2 tsp coriander powder

pinch of salt

Makhani Gravy

500 g tomatoes, chopped

2 garlic cloves, crushed

2 green chillies, left whole

4 cardamom pods, bruised

1/4 tsp clove powder

250 ml water

1 tsp garam masala

1 tsp fenugreek powder

pinch of salt

lots of chopped coriander

This thali is made up of Paneer Tawa Masala, Brinjal Bhaji, Green Vegetable and Potato Mallung, Coconut Sambal, Coriander and Mint Chutney and poppadoms.

Paneer Tawa Masala, spicy fried paneer

Fry the cubed paneer in the ghee until golden on all sides. Remove from pan and set aside.

Add the ajowan seeds to the ghee and stir-fry until they pop, then add the onion and fry until soft. Next add the ginger and green chillies and fry for 5 minutes.

Stir in the chilli powder, coriander powder and salt. Add the paneer and stir-fry for a minute. Leave to marinate whilst you make the Makhani Gravy.

Makhani Gravy

Put half the chopped tomatoes, the garlic paste, green chillies, cardamom pods, clove powder and water in a saucepan. Bring to the boil and simmer gently for 30 minutes or until the gravy is thick.

Add the paneer, the remaining tomatoes, the garam masala, fenugreek powder and salt. Stir and then cook for 5 minutes.

Check for seasoning and garnish with fresh chopped coriander.

Paneer is traditional Indian cheese, made from curds acidified with lemon juice. Raw, it has a rubbery tasteless quality, but when cooked it absorbs the cooking flavours, doesn't melt and is solid enough to hold together. Available from Asian stores.

Brinjal Bhaji

1 large aubergine

1 tbsp turmeric

1 tsp salt

3 tbsps sunflower oil

1 red onion, sliced

3 garlic cloves, chopped

1 thumb sized piece of fresh ginger root, peeled and chopped

1 large red chilli, sliced

1 tbsp brown mustard seed

1/2 tsp fenugreek

8 curry leaves

4 tomatoes, quartered

Green Vegetable and Potato Mallung

1 tbsp sunflower oil

1 medium onion, sliced

2 medium sized potatoes

250 g broccoli florets

250 g courgette, cut in chunks

175 g spinach, shredded

1 tsp brown mustard seeds

1/2 tsp fenugreek seeds, dry-roasted

1/2 tsp turmeric

4 small green chillies

1 stem lemongrass, bruised

8 curry leaves

3 cm piece of rampi

400 ml tin of coconut milk

1 tsp salt

Coriander and Mint Chutney

140 g fresh coriander

60 g fresh mint

3-4 hot green chillies

pinch of asafoetida

2 tbsps lime juice

pinch of salt

100 ml water

Brinjal Bhaji

Cut the aubergine into half moon shaped slices, rub over with turmeric and salt and fry in 2 tablespoons of the sunflower oil until soft. Set aside.

Fry the onion in the remaining sunflower oil until soft. Whiz the garlic, ginger and chilli in a mini food processor, add to the onions and stir-fry for a couple of minutes.

Dry-roast the fenugreek in a small frying pan until it begins to change colour, then crush with a pestle and mortar. Add the mustard seeds to the fenugreek and crush to a yellow paste.

Add the fenugreek and mustard paste and curry leaves to the onion mix and stir in. Mix in the fried aubergines and tomatoes, then add 150 ml of water, cover and simmer gently for 20 minutes.

Green Vegetable and Potato Mallung

Fry the onion in the sunflower oil until translucent, but not browned.

In a pestle and mortar crush the fenugreek and mustard seeds to a paste. Add these to the fried onion, together with the turmeric and the chillies and quickly stir-fry.

Peel the potatoes and slice into wedges. Add the potatoes, lemongrass, curry leaves, rampi, coconut milk and salt to the stir-fried mixture. Bring to the boil and simmer gently until the potatoes are almost cooked.

Then add the broccoli and courgettes and cook for another 10 minutes, finally, add the spinach, stir in and cook for a further 5 minutes. Check for seasoning.

Coriander and Mint Chutney

Whiz all the ingredients together in a food processor to a smooth, thick dip.

Ajowan (or carom) seeds are from the caraway family and have a strong thyme-like flavour.

Rampi is a long green palm-like leaf. Also known as pandanus/screw pine leaf, it is used for flavouring in Malay, Thai and south Indian food.

Coconut Sambal

Soak the coconut in the boiling water for 30 minutes.

Fry the onion in the sunflower oil until soft. Add the garlic, ginger and chilli and fry until fragrant. Add the black mustard seeds and turmeric and fry until the mustard seeds pop.

Add the lime juice, soft brown sugar, desiccated coconut and water. Simmer gently until the coconut is tender. You may need to add more water if the sambal becomes too thick. The consistency should be slightly runny but textured. Serve the sambal cold.

Poppadoms

Poppadoms are made from lentil flour and are vegan and gluten-free. The best way to cook them is to fry them in a little oil. Alternatively you can grill them, brushing them first with oil. My favourite variety is black pepper. They also come in garlic, chilli and plain.

To serve

Serve a portion of each dish on a thali plate, together with basmati rice and a few poppadoms on the side.

Coconut Sambal

50 g unsweetened desiccated coconut

150 ml boiling water

1 small onion, finely diced

1 tbsp sunflower oil

1 garlic clove, crushed

2 cm piece root ginger, peeled and grated

1 red chilli, finely sliced

1 tsp black mustard seeds

1/2 tsp turmeric

1/2 lime, juiced

1 tsp soft brown sugar

12 poppadoms

A tagine is a North African stew named after the traditional earthenware pot, with conical lid, that they are cooked in. They are always served on top of a large mound of steaming couscous.

Date and Aubergine Tagine
with Couscous with Toasted Almonds and Fresh Mint.

SERVES 4/6

2 tbsps olive oil

1 medium onion, chopped

3 garlic cloves, peeled and chopped

1 red chilli, halved and deseeded

1/2 tsp cumin seeds

1 tsp ground coriander

1 tsp paprika

1/2 tsp turmeric

1/2 cinnamon stick

1 bay leaf

1 large potato, peeled

600 ml boiling water

1 small aubergine

200 g squash

100 g dates, chopped in half

1 tbsp lemon juice

salt and fresh black pepper

chopped fresh parsley

Couscous

200 g couscous

300 ml boiling water

1 tbsp olive oil

1/2 tsp turmeric

50 g flaked almonds, toasted

chopped fresh mint

salt and freshly ground black pepper

Heat the olive oil in a wok or large casserole and fry the onion until translucent. Add the garlic, chilli and spices and stir-fry for a few minutes, until the spices are fragrant. Chop the potato into even sized pieces, add to the pan and stir-fry for a couple of minutes.

Pour in enough boiling water to cover the mixture. Bring back to the boil and simmer gently for 10 minutes.

Chop the aubergine and squash into even sized pieces and add these to the pan. Simmer until all the vegetables are tender and the sauce has thickened – about 10 minutes.

Add the dates, take off the heat and leave for a couple of hours to let the spices infuse the sweet dates.

Remove the cinnamon stick, chilli and bay leaf. Add the lemon juice and season with salt and freshly ground black pepper. Garnish with plenty of chopped fresh parsley.

Couscous with Toasted Almonds and Fresh Mint

Place the couscous in a large heat-proof bowl and mix in the turmeric. Pour on the boiling water, stir in the olive oil.

Leave to stand until all the water has been absorbed. Fluff up the couscous with a fork.

Season to taste and add the toasted almonds and chopped fresh mint.

To serve

Pile the couscous onto a serving dish and top with the tagine

Curries from southern Thailand, where coconut palms fringe the beaches, are often made with fresh coconut milk. This curry is flavoured with red curry paste, giving it a warm pink colour. It is chilli hot, so have the cold beers ready.

Thai Red Curry with Tofu

Wash and prepare all the vegetables. Heat the oil in a large saucepan and fry the onion until soft and translucent.

Stir in the red curry paste, turmeric, lemongrass and lime leaves and quickly stir-fry. Then add the coconut milk and bring to the boil, stirring all the time.

Add all the vegetables and the tofu and simmer gently until the vegetables are cooked. Add the lime juice, shoyu and season to taste with salt and freshly ground black pepper.

Remove the lemongrass before serving.

Cook the Thai fragrant rice according to the instructions on page 201. Mix in the coriander, lime zest and a pinch of salt.

To serve

Serve in deep bowls, with a mound of rice topped with the Thai red curry and garnished with Thai basil.

The red curry paste recipe is on page 189. If you haven't got time to make your own buy a vegetarian red curry paste, just check the ingredients, because most Thai curry pastes contain shrimps.

Thai basil, sometimes called holy basil, has a darker leaf than sweet basil and a sharper, more aromatic flavour. Thai basil is easy to grow or can be bought from Asian stores. As an alternative use sweet basil with some fresh mint added.

SERVES 4/6

250 g plain tofu, cubed

2 tbsps sunflower oil

1 large onion, finely sliced

2 tbsps red curry paste (see page 189)

1/2 tsp turmeric

1 quill lemongrass, bruised

2 lime leaves

400 g tin of coconut milk

1 carrot, sliced

1 red pepper, sliced

2 pak choy, roughly chopped

100 g baby sweetcorn

3 tomatoes, quartered

1 tbsp lime juice

1 tbsp shoyu

salt and freshly ground black pepper

a few sprigs of Thai basil, chopped for garnish

Thai fragrant rice, enough for 4

handful fresh coriander, chopped

zest of 1 lime

pinch of salt

◆ VEGAN ◆

LIGHT MEALS

Tarts

The most important part is the pastry case. Follow our technique for success every time

Salads

Colourful, original, unusual and refreshing ideas from warm to cold

Roasted Vegetables

The most simple, nutritious and colourful way to cook all sorts of vegetables

Tarts

Call it a flan, a quiche or a topless pie, a tart is an open pastry case made with a rich buttery shortcrust pastry and then filled with a savoury or sweet filling.

The Spanish call them 'tarta', the Italians 'torta' and the French 'tarte'. They are all basically the same and can be served hot or cold. They're great for picnics or those summer days when you want something to pull out of your fridge to quickly serve with a light salad.

The most important part of any tart is the pastry, and our recipe for this overleaf, if followed to the letter, will enable you to produce faultless tarts of your own time and time again. Conversely, you could of course buy some frozen shortcrust pastry, but it definitely won't have the crispy, buttery, rich quality of this homemade one.

The secret of a good pastry is to make it on a cool surface in a cool place, with cool hands and with chilled ingredients straight from the fridge.

Great pastry will certainly ensure that your tart has a better than even chance of success, but it will also be judged by your filling. You can adapt any of these fillings to the ingredients that you have available. Experiment and you may enjoy them even more!

Pastry Making Techniques

This is a very simple method for making the shortcrust pastry that is used in several of the recipes that follow. The secret is to make sure that you keep everything cool. Take the butter or margarine straight from the fridge and use ice-cold water. Make the pastry in a cool part of the kitchen, ideally on a marble slab, and if you have hot hands, run them under cold water and dry them before handling the pastry.

Method

Pre-heat the oven to 190°C/Gas 5 and grease a 25 cm loose-bottomed tart tin.

You can either make the pastry by hand or in a food processor.

By hand

To make the pastry by hand: sieve the flour into a large bowl. Dice the butter or margarine and add to the flour and rub the fat into the flour with your finger tips until it resembles breadcrumbs.

Add the cold water a little at a time and gently knead until the pastry forms a soft ball.

Remove from the bowl, wrap in clingfilm and leave to rest in the fridge for at least 30 minutes.

In a food processor

To make the pastry in a food processor: place the flour in the food processor. Dice the butter and add to the flour and mix until it resembles breadcrumbs.

Add the cold water a little at a time and mix for only a few seconds until the pastry forms a soft ball.

Remove from the processor, wrap in clingfilm and leave to rest in the fridge for at least 30 minutes.

Rolling out

On a well-floured work surface roll out the pastry to 3 mm thick into a circular shape a little bigger than the tart tin.

Roll up the pastry onto your rolling pin and gently unroll the pastry over the tart tin. Ease the pastry into the tin, pushing it into the sides without stretching it, as it will shrink back when it cooks. Trim the edges around the rim and fill any holes with spare pastry, sticking them well in so that the filling can't escape. Prick the base all over with a fork.

Baking blind

Baking a pastry case 'blind' means cooking it with no filling. In the restaurant we use dried red kidney beans, which we bake over and over again. You can buy special ceramic balls for baking blind from kitchen shops.

Line the pastry case with silver foil or baking parchment so that the silver foil covers the whole case. Fill with dried beans and bake 'blind' in the pre-heated oven for 12–15 minutes.

Remove from the oven and leave to cool for a few minutes. Lift out the silver foil and remove the beans, keeping these to use again. Put the pastry case back in the oven for a further 5 minutes, or until the base is cooked. Then fill with your chosen filling and bake until set.

A rich French-style tart with a toasted hazelnut pastry, filled with mangetout, slices of green apple and topped with a cartwheel pattern of creamy Camembert.

Camembert, Mangetout and Apple Tart
with Hazelnut Pastry

Pre-heat the oven to 190°C/Gas 5.

Grease a 25 cm loose-bottomed tart tin.

Make the pastry and bake the case 'blind' by following the pastry making method given on page 134, adding the crumbled hazelnuts when you have reached the breadcrumb stage of the pastry.

To make the filling

Lightly fry the red onions in olive oil until just soft. Add the mangetout peas and stir-fry for a couple of minutes. Then add the apple and lemon juice and stir-fry for another couple of minutes.

Whisk together the eggs, double cream and milk, season well. Fill the pastry case with the vegetables, top with slices of Camembert in a cartwheel pattern and pour over the egg mixture. Bake in the pre-heated oven for 20 minutes or until set and golden.

Pastry

100 g plain white organic flour

50 g salted butter, diced

60 g hazelnuts, toasted, skins rubbed off and roughly processed

water to mix

Filling

2 medium red onions, thinly sliced

1 tbsp olive oil

100 g mangetout peas, topped, tailed and cut in half

1 green dessert apple, thinly sliced

1 tbsp lemon juice

3 eggs

150 ml double cream

50 ml milk

100 g Camembert, cut into thin slices

salt and freshly ground black pepper

This tart has an Italian twist, flavoured with creamy blue-veined Dolcelatte, and is best made in late May when asparagus is in season.

Broccoli, Asparagus and Dolcelatte Tart

SERVES 4/6

Pastry

150 g plain white organic flour

50 g butter, cut into cubes

25 g Cheddar cheese, grated

1 egg yolk

1 tbsp cold water

Filling

1 small head of broccoli (250 g)

250 g asparagus

3 eggs

100 g mascarpone

100 g Dolcelatte

2 tbsps fresh dill, chopped

salt and freshly ground black pepper

Pre-heat the oven to 190°C/Gas 5 and grease a 25 cm loose-bottomed tart tin.

Make the pastry following the pastry making method given on page 134, adding the grated cheese and egg yolk when you have reached the breadcrumb stage of the pastry, then bake 'blind'.

To make the filling

Cut the florets off the broccoli stalk and set aside. Chop up the best of the stalk and place in a saucepan.

Cut the tips off the asparagus at about 6 cm and set aside. Chop the best of the rest of the asparagus, discarding any woody bits and add to the broccoli stalk. Cover with water, bring to the boil and simmer until cooked. Drain and leave to cool.

Steam the broccoli florets and the asparagus tips until just tender, refresh under cold water and set aside.

Meanwhile, in the food processor whiz the eggs, mascarpone, Dolcelatte and dill. Add the drained broccoli stalk and asparagus stems and whiz to a glorious green colour and creamy texture. Season with salt and lots of freshly ground black pepper.

Pour the egg and cheese mixture into the pastry case and decorate with the broccoli florets and the asparagus tips. Bake in a pre-heated oven for about 20 minutes or until set and golden.

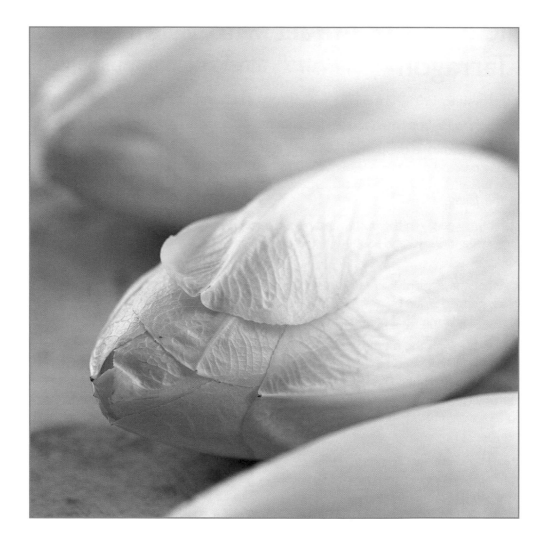

Salads

A great salad is simple, fresh, vital, raw and healthy. They have been part of the English diet since the 14th century when they were known as 'sallet'. They can be a meal in themselves rather than an adjunct to a main dish.

There is no point using wilted, tired, second rate or tasteless ingredients. As in all cooking, the quality of the ingredients is central, so buy the freshest vegetables you can. For guaranteed freshness grow your own salad leaves – rocket, lambs lettuce, mitsuna, purslane, buckler leaf, sorrel – in window boxes. For colour grow edible flowers such as nasturtiums, marigolds and pansies.

Essentially we eat with our eyes and as colour is so important, go for brightness and contrast in the ingredients that you use.

Don't forget the dressing, the simplest of tossed salad leaves can be turned around by a lively dressing. Get out your best single estate extra virgin olive oil, your 12 year old balsamic vinegar or a nutty pumpkin or walnut oil.

Each of the salads that follow has its own dressing, but it's worth having a feisty balsamic vinaigrette always made up (see page 186). Unless it's a marinated salad, dress just before serving.

An unusual salad with the bitterness of the chicory and radicchio balanced by the sweetness of the raspberries. The combination of colours in this salad looks great on the plate.

Raspberry and Ginger Tofu Salad
with Chicory and Radicchio Leaves and a Raspberry Vinaigrette

SERVES 4

250 g plain tofu, drained and cut into 5 cm x 2 cm strips

Marinade

½ orange, juiced

1 tbsp sherry

1 tbsp tamari

1 tsp apple juice concentrate

2 cm fresh root ginger, grated and the juice squeezed out

Raspberry Vinaigrette

100 ml extra virgin olive oil

50 ml raspberry vinegar

1 tsp apple juice concentrate

1 tbsp fresh coriander, chopped

salt and freshly ground black pepper

100 g fresh raspberries

1 radicchio

1 chicory

Pre-heat the oven to 200°C/Gas 6.

Marinade

Make the marinade and marinate the tofu for 30 minutes. Drain and retain the marinade to use again.

Lightly oil a baking dish, add the tofu and bake in the pre-heated oven until golden and crisp, turn the tofu often for an even tan.

Crush half the raspberries, retain the other half for decoration.

Raspberry Vinaigrette

Mix the dressing ingredients together and add the crushed raspberries.

To serve

Fill a salad bowl with radicchio and chicory leaves. Pile on the baked tofu, drizzle on the raspberry vinaigrette and decorate with the fresh raspberries.

A typical Provençal salad, usually made with anchovies and tuna, but we use capers instead to give the salad a similar distinctive taste.

Niçoise Salad

SERVES 4

400 g baby new potatoes

160 g French beans, topped and tailed

400 g tin sugar free cannellini beans

100 g pitted black olives

50 ml capers, drained

handful of fresh parsley, chopped

4 eggs, hardboiled and quartered

freshly ground black pepper

Tomato and Basil Dressing

100 ml extra virgin olive oil

1 garlic clove, crushed

1 tbsp wine vinegar

1 tbsp balsamic vinegar

1 tsp tomato purée

1 tsp apple juice concentrate

1 tsp lemon juice

1 tbsp fresh basil, chopped

pinch of salt

freshly ground black pepper

Boil the potatoes until just cooked. Leave to cool.

Steam the French beans and then refresh in cold water, drain and mix with the potatoes.

Drain and rinse the cannellini beans and mix them in with the potatoes and French beans. Stir in the olives, capers and parsley. Top with the quartered boiled eggs.

Tomato and Basil Dressing

Whisk all the ingredients together.

To serve

Pour the tomato and basil dressing over the salad and twist on some black pepper. Serve with slices of toasted French bread.

This very simple summer salad recipe was given to me when I ate at the Casa Luna restaurant in Ubud, in Bali — a wonderful haven owned by an Australian.

Avocado Sol
with a Yoghurt and Lemongrass Dressing

First make the dressing, it's quick to make.

Yoghurt and Lemongrass Dressing

In a small saucepan simmer the lemongrass in the apple and lemon juice for 5 minutes until the liquid has reduced by half to a thick syrup, take off the heat, remove the lemongrass and leave to cool completely.

When cool stir in the yoghurt, add the turmeric and season to taste.

When the dressing is cold, prepare the avocados and melon. Add the cherry tomatoes and spoon on the yoghurt and lemongrass dressing.

To serve

Serve at once, as the avocado will discolour very quickly. Put the Avocado Sol on a bed of shredded little gem lettuce.

You will have some yoghurt and lemongrass dressing left over, but it keeps well in the fridge and is delicious as a dressing for green leaf salads.

SERVES 4

2 avocados, peeled and cubed

1 cantaloupe melon, peeled and cubed

200 g cherry tomatoes, halved

Yoghurt and Lemongrass Dressing

1 stick lemongrass, bruised

200 ml apple juice

1 tbsp lemon juice

125 g vegan yoghurt

pinch of turmeric

salt and freshly ground black pepper

1 little gem lettuce

♦ VEGAN ♦

Our version of a Tuscan bread salad in which, traditionally, the bread is soaked in the salad. At Demuths we found the result too soggy with the bread soaked in it, so we serve it with ciabatta chilli croutons instead.

Panzanella Salad

SERVES 4

250 g aubergines, cut into bite sized chunks

olive oil for roasting

Marinade

4 garlic cloves, finely chopped

150 ml red grape juice

50 ml red wine

25 ml lemon juice

1 tbsp tomato purée

1 tbsp fresh basil, chopped

freshly ground black pepper

Salad

6 tomatoes, cut in eighths

1 red pepper, sliced

salt and freshly ground black pepper

Croutons

1/3 of a ciabatta loaf

50 ml olive oil

1/2 tsp cayenne

1/2 tsp paprika

Garnish

1 medium red onion, peeled and thinly sliced into rings

extra virgin olive oil for drizzling

fresh basil, chopped

This recipe needs to be made in two parts, with the aubergines left to marinate overnight.

Pre-heat the oven to 225°C/Gas 7.

In a lightly oiled baking tin, roast the aubergine in the pre-heated oven until tender and beginning to brown. Decant the aubergines into a bowl.

Marinade

Mix the marinade together, pour this over the aubergines and leave them to marinate overnight.

Salad

The next day, make up the tomato and pepper salad and mix in the marinated aubergines.

Croutons

Slice the ciabatta into 1 cm slices and cut each slice in half. Fry the ciabatta croutons in the olive oil, drain them on kitchen paper and sprinkle with cayenne and paprika.

To serve

To serve, top the salad with onion rings and hot chilli croutons. Drizzle with olive oil and sprinkle with chopped fresh basil.

◆ VEGAN ◆

Green Papaya Salad is very refreshing in the heat of Laos, where it is served with a liberal amount of very hot red birds-eye chillies. For this version I have toned down the chilli content.

Laotian Green Papaya Salad

SERVES 4/6

½ green papaya (250 g), peeled and grated

50 g cashew nuts, roasted

2 garlic cloves, finely chopped

1 red chilli, finely chopped

1 lime, juice and zest

½ tbsp brown sugar

2 tomatoes, finely chopped

2 spring onions, finely chopped

1 tbsp Thai basil, finely chopped

Peel and grate the papaya into a large bowl, discarding the seeds.

Roast the cashew nuts in the oven until they are a pale golden colour. This should only take a few minutes. Watch out, as they are very easy to burn.

Chop the garlic and chilli and pummel to a paste either in a mortar or whiz in a mini food processor. Add the lime zest, juice and sugar to the chilli paste and mix in with the grated papaya.

Very finely chop the tomatoes and spring onions and mix into the salad.

To serve

Pile the salad into a serving bowl. Season with salt and freshly ground black pepper and decorate with chopped basil and roasted cashew nuts.

Green papayas are not sweet and have the texture of a firm marrow, but with much lower water content. Green papayas are generally only available from Asian stores.

Thai basil, sometimes called holy basil, has a darker leaf than sweet basil and a sharper, more aromatic flavour. Thai basil is easy to grow but you can buy it from Asian stores. Otherwise use sweet basil with some fresh mint added.

◆ VEGAN ◆

This is a small starter sized salad, served on individual plates. Very quick to make and the classic combination of the pear and the blue cheese is delicious. The hot dressing makes it an ideal winter salad.

Pear and Blue Cheese Salad
with Hot Walnut and Honey Dressing

Arrange the lettuce leaves on the plates and decorate with watercress. Fan out the pear halves on top of the leaves and crumble over the blue cheese.

Dressing

Toss the walnuts in a small frying pan over a medium heat until fragrant. Add the olive oil, lemon juice and honey and heat enough for the honey to melt.

To serve

Pour the hot dressing over the pears and serve at once with some nutty three seed bread.

SERVES 4

frilly lettuce leaves

sprigs of watercress

2 pears, peeled, each one cut in half, depipped and fanned out

100 g blue cheese, crumbled

Dressing

100 g walnuts, toasted in a small frying pan

100 ml extra virgin olive oil

1 tbsp lemon juice

1 tbsp honey

This is a very nourishing salad packed with tofu, lentils, avocado and sunflower seeds. It has an oil free dressing which is a little different.

Smoked Tofu, Puy Lentil and Spinach Salad
with Apple and Tamari Dressing

SERVES 4

100 g puy lentils

1 tsp vegetable bouillon powder

1 bay leaf

200 g smoked tofu, sliced in fingers

baby spinach leaves

1 avocado, thinly sliced

12 cherry tomatoes, halved

50 g green pitted olives

50 g beansprouts, washed

4 tbsps tamari roasted sunflower seeds

fresh chives, chopped, for garnish

Apple and Tamari Dressing

200 ml apple juice

50 ml tamari

2 cm knob ginger root, grate and add the juice to the dressing

1 tbsp apple juice concentrate

First cook the puy lentils. Wash them thoroughly, cover with water, stir in the vegetable bouillon powder and add the bay leaf, bring to the boil, turn down the heat and simmer until the lentils are just cooked. Drain them and set aside.

Roast the sunflower seeds in a dash of sunflower oil and a tablespoon of tamari. It is worth making more tamari roasted sunflower seeds than you need for this recipe, as they keep well in an airtight container and are great with all kinds of rice and vegetables or just as a snack.

Apple and Tamari Dressing

This oil free dressing is so simple to make, just mix all the ingredients together.

To serve

I like to arrange this salad on individual plates. On each plate make a bed of spinach leaves, top with a few spoonfuls of puy lentils, share out the smoked tofu, decorate with slices of avocado, cherry tomatoes and green olives, sprinkle with beansprouts and tamari roasted sunflower seeds, pour on the dressing and garnish with chives.

Serve with organic wholewheat bread for a complete meal.

Taifun is my favourite make of smoked tofu but if you are unable to find it use Cauldron tofu instead.

Tamari is a naturally fermented, dark, strong soya sauce made from soya beans, salt and water. It is gluten-free and about twice as strong as shoyu.

◆ **VEGAN** ◆

This is my partner Nicho's creation, hence the scanty method, but notwithstanding that, it is the addition of the sesame oil that gives it such an unusual taste.

Mesquite Bean Salad

SERVES 4

4 tomatoes, diced

1 red pepper, diced

1 yellow pepper, diced

1 small red onion, peeled and diced

1 red chilli, thinly sliced

400 g tin sugar free mixed beans, drained and rinsed

Dressing

2 tbsps extra virgin olive oil

1 tbsp toasted sesame oil

1 tbsp tomato purée

1 tbsp tamari

1 tbsp lemon juice

1 tbsp apple juice concentrate

1 tsp paprika

salt and freshly ground black pepper

lots of fresh coriander, chopped

rocket leaves

watercress

In a salad bowl, mix the diced tomatoes, red and yellow peppers, red onion and chilli together. Add the mixed beans and stir in the dressing.

Dressing

To make the dressing whisk the olive oil, toasted sesame oil, tomato purée, tamari, lemon juice, apple juice concentrate and paprika together. Season with salt and freshly ground black pepper and add a good handful of fresh chopped coriander.

To serve

Serve with a dark green, peppery leaf salad made with rocket and watercress.

Caesar salad is traditionally made with anchovies, but as with the Nicoise salad we use capers instead for that vital piquancy. Mike, our greengrocer, suggested deep-frying the capers, which is a superb twist.

Caesar Salad
with Caesar Dressing

Remove the crusts from the bread and cut into small cubes. Heat a light olive oil in a small pan and fry the croutons until golden, then drain on kitchen paper.

Drain the capers and dry them thoroughly in kitchen paper to stop them spitting when you put them in the hot oil. Shallow-fry for a minute in a light olive oil – they will open up like flowers. Then drain them on kitchen paper.

Boil the eggs, just less than hardboiled, so that the yolks remain bright yellow.

In a salad bowl shred the lettuces, add the halved cherry tomatoes and top with the Parmesan slivers, croutons, deep-fried capers and hard-boiled eggs.

Caesar Dressing

This dressing is the essential ingredient in any Caesar salad, simply mix all the ingredients together.

To serve

Drizzle the dressing on the salad and decorate with chives.

Worcestershire sauce is traditionally flavoured with anchovies, but you can buy a vegetarian version from wholefood shops.

SERVES 4

100 g croutons

light olive oil for frying

4 tbsps capers, shallow-fried

4 hardboiled eggs, quartered

1 cos lettuce, thickly shredded

1 radicchio, thickly shredded

12 cherry tomatoes, halved

100 g vegetarian Parmesan cheese, sliced

8 tbsps Caesar dressing

fresh chives, chopped, for decoration

Caesar Dressing

1 garlic clove, crushed

1 tbsp capers

1 tbsp lemon juice

1 tsp vegetarian Worcestershire sauce

1 tsp fine herb mustard

1/4 tsp Tabasco

15 ml mayonnaise

freshly ground black pepper

Gado Gado is an Indonesian steamed vegetable salad with boiled eggs, salad garnishes and warm satay sauce. The essential ingredient is the satay, a spicy peanut sauce. You can vary the vegetables depending on what's in season.

Gado Gado Salad
with Satay Sauce

SERVES 4

2 tomatoes, diced

1 bunch spring onions, sliced

1/2 green pepper, thinly sliced

1/4 Chinese cabbage, shredded

100 g beansprouts, rinsed

1 tsp sesame seeds, toasted

Steamed Vegetables

100 g small new potatoes, cut in half

100 g carrots, peeled and cut into matchsticks

100 g broccoli, cut into small florets

100 g cauliflower, cut into small florets

75 g green beans, topped and tailed

a pinch of salt

200 ml Satay Sauce (see over for ingredients)

Prepare a salad from the tomatoes, spring onion, pepper, cabbage, beansprouts and toasted sesame seeds. Mix together well.

Steamed Vegetables

Boil the potatoes in salted water until cooked. Steam the rest of the vegetables until they are just cooked, but still have a bite to them. Mix the potatoes with the steamed vegetables and keep warm.

Satay Sauce

The easiest way to make Satay Sauce is in the food processor.

Blend the onion, garlic, chilli and ginger to a fine pulp in the food processor and then transfer this mixture to an oiled, thick-bottomed saucepan and fry for a few minutes, stirring all the time to prevent the onion pulp sticking.

Put the peanut butter, creamed coconut, lemon juice, shoyu, brown sugar and apple juice into the food processor and blend to a smooth porridge-like consistency, adding water if necessary.

Add the peanut mixture to the onion mixture in the saucepan and cook for a few minutes, stirring frequently.

To serve

Serve the Gado Gado on individual plates. Place a pile of steamed mixed vegetables in the middle of each plate, top with the salad and finish with a spoonful of hot Satay Sauce. Decorate the sides of the plates with the quartered hardboiled eggs and the sliced cucumber. Finally, sprinkle with chives and freshly ground black pepper.

Satay Sauce

1/2 onion, peeled and chopped

2 garlic cloves, peeled

1 green chilli, deseeded

2 cm fresh ginger root, peeled and chopped

450 g peanut butter

1/2 packet creamed coconut, chopped

1 lemon, juiced

75 ml shoyu

2 tbsps brown sugar

150 ml apple juice

Garnish

4 eggs, hardboiled and quartered

1/4 cucumber, sliced into half moon shapes

fresh chives, chopped

freshly ground black pepper

Any excess Satay Sauce will keep well in the fridge and is a delicious accompaniment to all manner of rice and vegetables.

Roasted Vegetables

This is the simplest, most nutritious and colourful way to cook all sorts of vegetables. Mediterranean countries base their cuisine around it.

You'll get a much better result if you heat an ovenproof dish with a little olive oil in it first. Add your vegetables, baste a little and then just place them in a hot oven.

During the cooking all you need do is stir them once or twice. When you take them out the vegetables will be tantalisingly aromatic and just beginning to caramelise.

Ever wondered what to do in the autumn and winter when squashes are varied and plentiful? It's easy. Just slice and roast them with chilli, lemon, sage leaves and generous chunks of fresh ginger.

Garlic bulbs can be roasted whole and have a softer, sweeter taste than when fried.

Red, yellow and orange peppers roasted until their skins blacken, peeled, sliced and served marinated and cold, make a lovely sweet salad. Cherry tomatoes with a splash of balsamic vinegar or asparagus simply roasted in olive oil with a sprinkling of coarse sea salt. They are all mouthwateringly tasty.

The idea for this recipe came from Chengdu, in Szechuan Province, western China where, for about £1, we were served 15 tiny plates of food on delicate blue and white flowery china, washed down with light green tea.

Roasted Peppers and Baby Broad Beans
with an Oriental Dressing

SERVES 4

150 g broad beans, depodded weight, peel if not very youthful

1 red pepper

1 orange pepper

1 yellow pepper

Dressing

1 tbsp tamari

1 tbsp rice wine vinegar

1 tbsp sunflower oil

2 tsps toasted sesame oil

1 tsp lemon juice

freshly ground black pepper

fresh coriander to garnish

Cook the broad beans in salted water until just tender. Drain and leave to cool.

Wash the peppers, cut in half, remove the seeds and roast under a hot grill until the skins are blackened. Place the peppers in a bowl and seal with cling film. Leave for 20 minutes. Take the peppers out of the bowl, peel off the skins, and slice thinly.

Mix the peppers and broad beans together. Pour on the dressing, mix well and leave to marinate.

Dressing

To make the dressing, mix all the ingredients together.

To serve

Serve with toasted ciabatta bread.

Fresh baby broad beans are so sweet and vibrantly green, but the season is very short, so it's not long before the broad beans become tough and starchy and you have to peel them.

1 kilo of fresh broad beans in the pod, when podded will end up at about 350 g. If they need peeling, you are then down to only 250 g.

◆ **VEGAN** ◆

Acorn squash has a firm, deep orange flesh that doesn't disintegrate when roasted. The lemon rind, honey and chilli give the roasted squash a Moorish sweet/hot flavour and the colours are fantastic.

Roasted Acorn Squash
with Lemon and Chilli

SERVES 4

100 ml olive oil

1 acorn squash, peeled and cut into bite sized slices

1 whole garlic bulb, the cloves peeled and left whole

1 red onion, sliced in segments

4 tomatoes, quartered

1 lemon, rind only, peeled with a potato peeler

1 dried ancho chilli, deseeded and shredded

1 tbsp shoyu

1 tsp brown sugar

freshly ground black pepper

Herb and Yoghurt Raita

125 g soya yoghurt

50 ml soya cream

plenty of fresh mint and coriander, finely chopped

salt and freshly ground black pepper

lambs lettuce for decoration

Pre-heat the oven to 200°C/Gas 6.

In a large baking tray, heat the olive oil in the oven. Add all the ingredients except the shoyu, sugar and pepper. Stir well so that all the vegetables are well coated in the olive oil.

Roast until the squash is just tender, and then add the shoyu, sugar and lots of black pepper, stir and roast for a further 5 minutes.

Herb and Yoghurt Raita

Mix all ingredients together and chill.

To serve

Serve with the cooling fresh Herb and Yoghurt Raita, either as a starter, decorated with lambs lettuce, or as a main meal, with nutty brown rice.

An ancho chilli is a dried poblano chilli. It's large, mild and richly flavoured and used in Mexican cooking.

Vegan yoghurt is made in exactly the same way as milk yoghurt, but using soya milk.

♦ VEGAN ♦

For me asparagus is the queen of vegetables, especially if eaten with your fingers. Ensure that it's as fresh as possible and that you only eat it in May and the beginning of June. It is so much better than white forced asparagus, which is tasteless, slimy and has no bite.

Griddled Asparagus
with *Salsa Verde*

The simplest way to cook asparagus is to griddle them. Cut off the woody ends, wash and put straight on a very, very hot griddle. It's essential that the griddle is smoking before putting on the asparagus.

Griddle for 2 minutes on one side and then turn over and griddle for 2 more minutes. The asparagus should be a brilliant green colour, with a touch of burnt.

Salsa Verde

Put everything in the food processor in the order given in the ingredients list, whizzing each time before adding the next ingredient. The mix should be runny, so add more olive oil if it starts to get too thick.

To serve

Serve the griddled asparagus at once, accompanied by the Salsa Verde and some warm crusty French bread.

If you don't have a griddle, try baking it in a hot oven with the asparagus rolled in olive oil and sprinkled with a little coarse sea salt.

SERVES 2/4

450 g asparagus

Salsa Verde

2 garlic cloves, peeled

50 g fresh mint, destalked

25 g fresh basil, destalked

½ bunch watercress, destalked

1 tbsp apple juice concentrate

1 tbsp white wine vinegar

125 ml extra virgin olive oil

♦ VEGAN ♦

You'll need three types of squash for this recipe. Onion squash, orange in colour with bright orange flesh. Crown prince squash, pale blue-green with paler orange flesh. Kabocha squash which has knobbly, dark green skin with pale green stripes and a dense orange flesh.

A Trio of Ginger Roasted Squash
with Whole Garlic and Wild Green Leaves

SERVES 4/6

¹/₂ onion squash

¹/₂ small crown prince

¹/₂ kabocha

12 whole garlic cloves, unpeeled

5 cm piece of fresh ginger

4 tbsps olive oil

2 tbsps tamari

Vegan Sour Cream

4 tbsps vegan yoghurt

2 tbsps vegan cream

1 tsp lemon juice

chopped fresh chives

freshly ground black pepper

rocket, for decoration

lambs lettuce, for decoration

mitsuna, for decoration

extra virgin olive oil and tamari to drizzle

Pick or buy squash in September when the flesh is still firm and sweet.

Mitsuna is a Japanese bitter leaf used as a herb.

Pre-heat the oven to 220°C/Gas 7.

Wash any mud off the squash and slice into 3 cm wide crescent moon shaped slices. Be careful when you slice the squash as the skin can be very hard to cut through. Using a large knife on a solid chopping board, first cut each squash in half, slice off the stem, scoop out the seeds and then slice. Leave the skin on as it's delicious when roasted.

Place the squash slices in one, or even two, large baking dishes, arranged so that they don't cover each other. Drizzle with extra virgin olive oil and tamari.

Scatter the whole, unpeeled garlic cloves over the squash. Grate the ginger and squeeze the ginger juice over the squash. Place in the pre-heated oven and bake until tender and beginning to brown.

Vegan Sour Cream

Mix the vegan yoghurt and cream together and then add the lemon juice, chives and black pepper.

To serve

Wash the rocket, lambs lettuce and mitsuna leaves and shake them dry. Decorate the plates with the leaves, drizzle with a little olive oil mixed with tamari and give each person one or two each of the different squash. Serve with Vegan Sour Cream.

The finest artichokes are French and the season starts in the middle of May. You can now buy artichokes from Spain all year round, but they often lack flavour. Choose ones that are plump with bright green-mauve leaves that haven't gone black at the tips.

Artichokes
with a Toasted Sesame Oil Dressing

Cut the stalks off the artichokes and wash well. You have a choice of cooking methods.

To roast, wrap each artichoke in silver foil and roast for 30 minutes in a hot oven.

To steam, put the artichokes stem ends down into the top of the steamer and steam for about 30 minutes or until the petals can be easily pulled out.

To boil, cover with water, bring to the boil and simmer for about 30 minutes until cooked. The length of cooking time depends on the size of the artichokes.

Toasted Sesame Oil Dressing

Whisk the olive oil, sesame oil and tamari together and season with a pinch of salt and freshly ground black pepper.

To serve

Drain and serve hot with the Toasted Sesame Oil Dressing poured over.

SERVES 2

2 globe artichokes

Toasted Sesame Oil Dressing

4 tbsps extra virgin olive oil

1 tsp toasted sesame oil

1 tsp tamari

salt and freshly ground black pepper

Food eaten with the fingers is far more enjoyable. Just provide lots of napkins and a large bowl to put the sucked petals in. The artichoke heart is the most delicious and has to be eaten last. Be careful to remove the choke, that's all the hairy bits, before eating the heart, because it can do exactly what its name suggests.

◆ VEGAN ◆

Puddings

We excel as a nation in our puddings. They are a very British institution. Sweet steamed puddings first found favour nationwide in the 17th century with the invention of the pudding cloth which replaced animal gut, which was previously only suitable for making savoury steamed puds.

In the rest of Europe puddings tended to be light, fruit based and generally served on special occasions. In the Middle East, they are more often served with coffee rather than as part of a meal and in the Far East fruit is served at the end of the meal partly to clear the palate. The Indonesian Black Rice Pudding here is traditionally served at breakfast, but we serve it at lunch and dinner.

Seasonality is important, for in winter one yearns for hot, dark, sticky, rich puddings and in summer, cold, colourful and light ones with lots of fresh fruit.

Vegans quite often get a raw deal when it comes to puddings, but at Demuths we do our best to spoil them with our Sticky Toffee Pudding and Chocolate Fudge Cake.

Everyone loves them and there are a few recipes here with that little twist of something extra in them!

The cardamom, lime leaves and lemongrass add an exotic touch to these poached peaches. The redcurrants add a dash of colour.

Poached Peaches with Redcurrants
in a Cardamom, Lime Leaf and Lemongrass Syrup

SERVES 6

6 unblemished, not too ripe peaches

200 g redcurrants

250 g caster sugar

750 ml water

4 lime leaves

1 stalk lemongrass, bruised

8 cardamom pods, bruised

Into a stainless steel saucepan, put the caster sugar and water. Bring this to the boil and then simmer until the sugar has dissolved. Add the lime leaves, lemongrass and cardamom pods.

Put the whole peaches into the syrup. The syrup should almost cover the peaches, if it doesn't, top up with a little more water. Put a lid on the pan and simmer very gently, until the peaches are tender – the length of time they will need depends on how ripe they are. Test if they are cooked with the tip of a knife.

Leave the peaches to cool in the syrup for a short while, then take them out and peel them. Remove the stones and cut the peaches in half.

Take the stems off the redcurrants and rinse the berries.

Reheat the syrup and reduce by a half to a syrupy consistency. Remove the lime leaves, lemongrass and cardamom.

Add the redcurrants to the syrup and simmer for a couple of minutes, until the redcurrants just begin to burst. Turn off the heat.

To serve

Pour the redcurrant syrup over the peaches and serve warm or cold with vanilla soya ice-cream.

This Mocha Truffle Hazelnut Cake is very easy to make, just make sure the coffee is cold and the chocolate is very gently melted.

Mocha Truffle Hazelnut Cake

SERVES 8

150 g digestives

140 g hazelnuts, roasted

75 g unsalted butter, melted

425 ml whipping cream

50 g icing sugar, sieved

200 g dark chocolate, melted

1 tbsp cold espresso coffee

Either buy ready roasted de-skinned hazelnuts or roast the hazelnuts in a hot oven until golden and then rub off the skins.

Grease a 25 cm sponge tin with a removable bottom and line with baking parchment.

Place the digestives and roasted hazelnuts in a food processor and whiz to a breadcrumb consistency. Add the melted butter and mix in. The mix should be of a consistency to form a ball.

Press into the prepared sponge tin and leave to set.

Make a really strong espresso coffee and leave to cool.

Whip the cream and fold in the icing sugar.

Melt the chocolate in a bain-marie or in the microwave on defrost setting. When it's just melted leave to cool a little and then fold into the whipped cream. Add a tablespoon of cold espresso coffee and fold in.

Spoon the mixture over the biscuit base and refrigerate until set.

To serve

Serve cold, with whipped cream and a dusting of chocolate.

A traditional recipe for Crème Brûlée, spiced up with rhubarb and ginger.

Crème Brûlée
with a Rhubarb and Ginger Filling

You will need 6 x 100 ml ramekins.

Rhubarb and Ginger Filling

First make the rhubarb mixture by cooking the rhubarb with the sugar, stem ginger and a tablespoon of the syrup from the stem ginger jar. Leave to cool.

Heat the double cream in a saucepan until it reaches boiling point and transfer to a jug.

Whisk the egg yolks with the cornflour, caster sugar and vanilla essence in a large bowl. Pour the hot cream very slowly into the egg mixture, whisking all the time. Return the mixture to the saucepan or into a double boiler and heat gently, stirring all the time, until you have thick custard. Transfer the custard to a jug.

Cover the base of each ramekin with a 1cm thick layer of the rhubarb and ginger mixture, then pour over the custard, leaving enough room at the top for the burnt sugar topping. Any leftover rhubarb and ginger mixture is delicious eaten with Greek yoghurt.

Cover each ramekin with clingfilm and refrigerate overnight.

Topping

To caramelise the custards, grind the sugar in an electric grinder and sieve the sugar over the chilled custards. Place the custards under a very hot grill until the sugar bubbles and begins to brown. Take them out from under the grill and add another thin layer of sugar and grill again to an even darker brown caramel.

Let them stand for a couple of minutes while the caramel hardens and then serve at once. If you caramelise the custards in advance and put them in the fridge the sugar melts after about an hour.

SERVES 6

570 ml double cream

3 drops pure vanilla essence

6 egg yolks

4 tsps cornflour, level

2 tbsps caster sugar

Rhubarb and Ginger Filling

1 stick of rhubarb, chopped

1 tbsp caster sugar

4 pieces stem ginger, finely chopped

Topping

110 g golden granulated sugar, ground

It is far easier caramelising the sugar with a blowtorch and you also get a better result. Kitchen shops now sell miniature blowtorches for this very purpose.

This is our vegan recipe for Sticky Toffee Pudding. The quantities for the toffee sauce are large, but that's the best part of a Sticky Toffee Pudding.

Sticky Toffee Pudding

SERVES 4

250 ml soya milk

100 ml water

200 g dates

1 level tsp bicarbonate of soda

115 g vegan margarine

115 g soft brown sugar

200 g white self-raising flour

1/8 tsp ground nutmeg

1/4 tsp ground ginger

1/4 tsp ground cinnamon

Toffee Sauce

100 g golden syrup

200 g soft brown sugar

150 g vegan margarine

100 ml soya cream

1 tsp pure vanilla essence

Pre-heat the oven to 190°C/Gas 5.

Line a 20 cm × 20 cm shallow cake tin with baking parchment.

Chop the dates in half, put them in a small saucepan and cover with the soya milk and water. Simmer until the dates are soft. Take off the heat and stir in the bicarbonate of soda, which will froth as you add it to the date mixture. Leave to cool.

Beat together the margarine and sugar until pale and creamy. Add the date mixture and stir in.

Mix the spices into the flour. Sieve the flour and fold into the sponge mixture. Spoon the sponge mixture into the prepared tin.

Bake in the pre-heated oven for 30 minutes or until cooked and the sponge bounces back when pressed.

Toffee Sauce

Melt the syrup, margarine, sugar and vanilla essence in a small saucepan and simmer for 5 minutes without stirring. Leave to cool slightly and then stir in the soya cream.

To serve

Prick the pudding all over and pour half the hot toffee sauce over the pudding. Serve the rest of the sauce with the pudding and, if you like, a scoop of vanilla soya ice-cream.

This is a very rich festive tart and a great alternative to Christmas pudding. Fresh cranberries are usually only available at Christmas, but alternatives are puréed plums, apricots, gooseberries and blackcurrants.

Cranberry and Almond Bakewell Tart

SERVES 8

300 g plain white flour

150 g butter, diced

50 g icing sugar

2 egg yolks

1 tbsp cold water

Fruit Layer

340 g fresh cranberries

100 g Demerara sugar

1 piece cinnamon stick

water, just enough to cover the cranberries

Almond Topping

300 g unsalted butter, in small cubes

300 g caster sugar

300 g ground almonds

3 eggs

flaked almonds to sprinkle on top

Unsalted butter is essential for the almond topping and is best for all puddings, as there is nothing worse than a sweet over-salted pudding.

Pre-heat the oven to 180°C/Gas 4.

For the pastry, put the flour and butter in a food processor and whiz until the mixture resembles breadcrumbs. Add the sugar, whiz again and then add the egg yolks and water, adding more water if the mix is too dry. Mix to a soft-ball consistency and refrigerate for one hour.

Grease a 30 cm loose-bottomed flan dish and roll out the pastry to fill the dish. Bake 'blind' (see page 134) and then leave to cool.

Fruit Layer

Rinse the cranberries, picking out any bad ones and then boil them up with the sugar, cinnamon stick and just enough water to cover. Simmer until the berries have popped and the fruity mixture is thick – about 30 minutes. The mixture needs to be on the tart side to contrast with the sweet almond topping. Leave to cool.

Almond Topping

Put the butter in a food processor with the caster sugar and mix to a creamy white consistency. Add the ground almonds and eggs and whiz to a smooth paste.

Spread the cranberries over the base of the pastry case. Then spoon on the almond topping and smooth it out with a palette knife. Sprinkle with flaked almonds. Bake for 30 minutes at 200°C/Gas 6 until pale golden and puffy.

To serve

Eat warm with lots of cream.

Vegans usually get a raw deal when it comes to cakes and puddings that require eggs to make them rise. This is an exception. This cake can be iced or served warm as a pudding with Hot Chocolate Sauce.

Chocolate Fudge Cake
with Hot Chocolate Sauce

Pre-heat the oven to 190°C/Gas 5.

Grease and line a 20 cm cake tin with baking parchment.

Sift the flour, baking powder and cocoa into a large mixing bowl. Add the caster sugar, vanilla essence, sunflower oil, orange juice and water. Whisk to a batter-like consistency and pour into the prepared tin.

Bake in the middle of the pre-heated oven for approximately 40 minutes or until a skewer comes out clean when inserted into the cake.

Hot Chocolate Sauce

Sift the icing sugar and the cocoa into a bowl. Melt the margarine with the boiling water. Add the margarine mixture to the sugar mixture and mix well.

Use either as a hot sauce poured over slices of the cake, or as a cold icing. The sauce will harden as it cools, so if you want an icing spread the warm topping over the cake and leave to set.

To serve

As a pudding, serve slices of the Chocolate Fudge Cake warm with the Hot Chocolate Sauce poured over, together with a large scoop of vanilla soya ice-cream.

SERVES 8

300 g self-raising flour

3 tsps baking powder

50 g cocoa

250 g caster sugar

1 tsp pure vanilla essence

9 tbsps sunflower oil

175 ml orange juice

175 ml water

Hot Chocolate Sauce

250 g icing sugar

1 tbsp cocoa

50 g vegan sunflower margarine

3 tbsps boiling water

◆ VEGAN ◆

My mother made hazelnut meringues, with fresh raspberries in summer and chestnut purée in winter. I remember, as a child, I was once blamed for licking the cream out of the meringues whilst guests were eating their first course in the dining room. It was actually the cat!

Hazelnut Meringues
with *Fresh Strawberries and Crème Fraîche*

SERVES 6

3 egg whites
175 g caster sugar
50 g ground hazelnuts
150 ml whipping cream
150 ml crème fraîche
350 g fresh strawberries
icing sugar to dust
roasted hazelnuts to decorate

Pre-heat the oven to 140°C/Gas 1.

Line 2 baking sheets with non-stick baking parchment and draw a 20 cm circle on both sheets.

Whisk the egg whites until stiff and gradually add the caster sugar, whisking between each addition. Very carefully fold in the ground hazelnuts with a large metal spoon, do not whisk.

Divide the mixture between the baking sheets and spread out evenly with a spatula within the circle that you have drawn on the baking parchment.

Place in the centre of the pre-heated oven and cook for 1 ½ hours. Leave to cool.

Whip the cream and stir in the crème fraîche. Spread one of the meringues with half the cream mixture and half the strawberries, place the other meringue on top and spread with the rest of the cream mixture and decorate with the remaining strawberries. Sift over the icing sugar and sprinkle with roasted hazelnuts.

The secret to lily-white meringues is a long slow cook in a very cool oven, one knack is to turn the oven off and leave the meringues in overnight.

Fill the meringues with the strawberries and cream just before eating, otherwise the meringue goes soggy or the cat nicks the cream.

This is our version of the River Cafe's recipe Crostada di Limone. It is made with limes, bulked out with desiccated coconut, but is not as extravagant. In truth it is a glorification of a curd tart.

Lime, Lemon and Coconut Tart

SERVES 12

300 g plain white flour, sieved

150 g unsalted butter, diced

50 g icing sugar

2 egg yolks

1 tbsp cold water

Lime, Lemon and Coconut Filling

4 limes and 1 lemon, finely grated zest and juice

4 whole eggs

6 egg yolks

300 g caster sugar

250 g unsalted butter, softened

100 g desiccated coconut

Pre-heat the oven to 180°C/Gas 4.

You will need a 30 cm loose-bottomed flan case, as this is a large tart, but for a smaller one cut the quantities in half. Grease the flan case.

To make the pastry, put the flour and the diced butter in a food processor and whiz until the mixture resembles breadcrumbs. Add the sugar, whiz again and then add the egg yolks and water. You may need a touch more water if the mix is too dry. Mix to a soft-ball consistency, and refrigerate for one hour.

On a lightly floured surface, roll out the pastry as thinly as possible. Roll the pastry up onto your rolling pin and carefully lay it over the flan dish. Press the pastry snugly into the flan case and trim any surplus from around the edges. Line with silver foil, making sure that the pastry edges are well covered. Fill with dried beans and place in the centre of the pre-heated oven to 'bake blind' for 15 minutes, following the instructions given on page 134.

Take the flan case out of the oven and leave it to rest for a couple of minutes before removing the silver foil and beans. Then put the flan case back in the oven for 5 minutes to dry out the base to an even, pale golden colour. Leave to cool.

Lime, Lemon and Coconut Filling

Whisk the eggs with the caster sugar in a large bowl. Then slowly add the lime, lemon juice and zest, whisking all the time. With so much citrus juice there is always a danger of curdling the mixture, so keep on whisking. Pour the mixture into a stainless steel saucepan or the top of a bain-marie and over a very low heat continue to whisk until the sugar has dissolved.

Use organic un-waxed limes and lemons, so that the zest is pure. You would be shocked at the amount of poisonous substances on your average sprayed dyed waxed citrus fruit.

Having got through 12 eggs, don't waste the egg whites, go pudding mad, and make hazelnut meringues (see recipe on page 176).

Add half the butter and continue to whisk. The mixture will begin to thicken as the eggs cook, it takes an age so be patient and don't be tempted to turn up the heat or you will end up with very expensive, sweet scrambled eggs. When the mixture is thick enough to coat the back of the spoon add the remaining butter and continue stirring until the mixture is thick and curd-like.

Stir in the desiccated coconut, pour into the pastry case, cover the edges with silver foil and bake in the pre-heated oven until set and golden – about 15 minutes.

To serve

Serve cold with a sprinkling of icing sugar, a slice of lime and a dollop of mascarpone.

This pudding has a wonderful nutty flavour and silky texture, with a striking contrast of colour between the blue-black of the rice and the creamy white of the coconut cream. In Bali it is called Bubuh Injin and is eaten for breakfast, served with fresh coconut milk.

Indonesian Black Rice Pudding
with Coconut Cream, Topped with Tropical Fruit and Coconut

SERVES 4/6

200 g black glutinous rice
1 litre water
50 g soft brown sugar
1 vanilla pod

Coconut Cream

150 ml coconut milk
1 tbsp white sugar
2 tbsps coconut cream

tropical fruit
toasted coconut

Soak the black rice for 12 hours, rinse and place in a saucepan with the water, sugar and vanilla pod. Bring to the boil and then simmer, uncovered, for 1 hour or until the rice is soft and all the water has been absorbed. The rice pudding should be thick and glossy.

Coconut Cream

To make the coconut cream, heat the coconut milk, coconut cream and sugar together until the sugar has dissolved.

To serve

Fill a bowl with warm black rice pudding and top with hot coconut cream, finish with sliced tropical fruit, such as mango, papaya or lychee and sprinkle with toasted coconut.

Black rice is a glutinous short grain black rice from Indonesia. You can buy this rice in Asian stores.

♦ VEGAN ♦

Basics

Tomato and Papaya Chutney ◆VEGAN◆

3 cm piece root ginger, peeled and chopped

2 garlic cloves, peeled

1 red chilli, finely sliced

1 tbsp sunflower oil

1 tsp punch puran

700 g tomatoes, cored and chopped

50 g dried apricots, chopped

100 g soft brown sugar

100 ml wine vinegar

¼ tsp salt

½ small papaya, peeled and chopped

Serve with Vedgeree (page 64). Serve as part of a thali or with sweet potato puri. This chutney is also great with hunks of bread and a tasty cheddar cheese.

This is a fresh chutney with not much sugar and just the sweetness from the fruit to preserve it. It will keep in the fridge well-covered for a couple of weeks. If you can't get papaya, mango is a good alternative.

Method: Whiz the ginger, garlic and chilli in a mini food processor to a chunky paste.

Heat the sunflower oil in a large saucepan, add the ginger mix and the punch puran and stir-fry until fragrant.

Add the tomatoes, apricots, sugar, vinegar and salt, stir and simmer gently for 30 minutes until it has reduced to a thick chutney consistency. Add the papaya and simmer for 5 minutes. Leave to cool.

Coconut Sambal ◆VEGAN◆

1 tsp soft brown sugar

50 g unsweetened desiccated coconut

1 small onion, finely diced

1 tbsp sunflower oil

1 garlic clove, crushed

2 cm piece root ginger, peeled and grated

1 red chilli, finely sliced

1 tsp black mustard seeds

½ tsp turmeric

½ lime, juiced

150 ml boiling water

Coconut Sambal is always served with thalis and is also a delicious accompaniment to all South Indian vegetable curries.

Method: Soak the coconut in the boiling water for 30 minutes. Fry the onion in the sunflower oil until soft. Add the garlic, ginger and chilli and fry until fragrant. Add the black mustard seeds and turmeric and fry until the mustard seeds pop.

Add the lime juice, soft brown sugar, desiccated coconut and water. Simmer gently until the coconut is tender. You may need to add more water if the sambal becomes too thick. The consistency should be slightly runny but textured. Serve the sambal cold.

Iranganis' Date Pickle ◆VEGAN◆

200 ml rice vinegar

200 ml water

2 garlic cloves, crushed

thumb sized piece of ginger, peeled and finely chopped

1/4 cinnamon stick

4 cardamom pods, crushed

2 tsps chilli powder

1 tsp mustard seeds, crushed

1 tsp salt

250 g pitted dates

4 tbsps brown sugar

Serve with vegetable curries such as Saag Paneer (page 114).

Method: In a stainless steel saucepan heat the vinegar and water and add the garlic, ginger, all the spices and the salt. Cover and simmer for 5 minutes.

Chop half the dates into small pieces and leave the rest whole. Add all of the dates and the sugar to the vinegar mix. Stir in and simmer very gently, uncovered, until the dates are soft – about 20 minutes. Leave to cool.

The pickle will keep forever and a day.

Coriander and Mint Chutney ◆VEGAN◆

140 g fresh coriander

60 g fresh mint

3-4 hot green chillies

pinch of asafoetida

2 tbsps lime juice

pinch of salt

100 ml water

Serve this chutney cold, as part of a thali (page 124).

Method: Whiz all the ingredients together in a food processor to a smooth, thick dip.

Cranberry Relish ◆VEGAN◆

SERVES 6/8

225 g fresh cranberries

4 cardamom pods

1/2 cinnamon stick

2 cloves

2 star anise

100 g caster sugar

1 lemon, peel and 1/2 the juice

This relish goes well with Christmas Roast (page 106) and is also delicious with Glamorgan Sausages (page 68).

Method: Place the cranberries in a saucepan and cover with water, but not enough to allow the berries to float.

Peel the lemon with a potato peeler. Add the spices and lemon peel to the cranberries and bring to the boil. Simmer slowly until about half the berries have popped. Stir in the sugar and lemon juice. Simmer on a low heat, stirring often, until all the sugar has dissolved. Serve cold.

Balsamic Dressing ◆VEGAN◆

200 ml extra virgin olive oil
50 ml balsamic vinegar
1 tbsp lemon juice
2 tsps apple juice concentrate
2 tsps whole grain mustard
salt and freshly ground black pepper

This is a classic salad dressing that I always keep made up in the kitchen, ready to drizzle on salad leaves or serve with roasted vegetables, artichokes and asparagus.

Method: Either by hand or in a food processor, mix the olive oil, balsamic vinegar, lemon juice, apple juice concentrate and mustard together.

Add sea salt and freshly ground black pepper to taste.

Apple and Tamari Dressing ◆VEGAN◆

200 ml apple juice
50 ml tamari
2 cm knob ginger root, grate and add the juice to the dressing
1 tbsp apple juice concentrate

This oil free dressing is so simple to make and is delicious with Smoked Tofu, Puy Lentil and Spinach Salad (page 152).

Method: Simply mix all the ingredients together.

Vegan Mayonnaise ◆VEGAN◆

135 ml soya milk
1½ tbsps cider vinegar
½ tbsp lemon juice
1½ tsps whole grain mustard
300 ml sunflower oil
salt and freshly ground black pepper

Serve as a dip with Wicked Cheese Chilli Rellenos (page 14), Roasted Squash (page 164) or with home-made chips.

Method: Place all the ingredients except the oil and the salt and pepper into the food processor. Blend until well mixed.

In exactly the same way as making classic mayonnaise, trickle the oil in very slowly whilst the food processor is running. The consistency of the mixture will gradually thicken as the oil is trickled in.

Finally, add sea salt and freshly ground black pepper to taste. This recipe makes 500 ml.

For garlic mayonnaise add 3 garlic cloves, for chilli mayonnaise add ½ teaspoon of smoked chilli powder.

Caesar Dressing

1 garlic clove, crushed
1 tbsp capers
1 tbsp lemon juice
1 tsp vegetarian Worcestershire sauce
1 tsp fine herb mustard
1/4 tsp Tabasco
15 ml mayonnaise
freshly ground black pepper

This dressing is the essential ingredient in Caesar Salad (page 155).

Method: Mix all the ingredients together.

Yoghurt and Lemongrass Dressing ◆VEGAN◆

1 stick lemongrass, bruised
200 ml apple juice
1 tbsp lemon juice
125 g vegan yoghurt
pinch of turmeric
salt and freshly ground black pepper

This dressing can be served with Avocado Sol (page 147), in salad wraps or with steamed vegetables. Or simply use it as a dressing for green leaf salads.

Method: In a small saucepan, simmer the lemongrass in the apple and lemon juice for 5 minutes or until the liquid has reduced by half to a thick syrup, take off the heat, remove the lemon grass and leave to cool completely.

When cool stir in the yoghurt, add the turmeric and season to taste.

Tomato and Basil Dressing ◆VEGAN◆

100 ml extra virgin olive oil
1 garlic clove, crushed
1 tbsp wine vinegar
1 tbsp balsamic vinegar
1 tsp tomato purée
1 tsp apple juice concentrate
1 tsp lemon juice
1 tbsp fresh basil, chopped
pinch of salt
freshly ground black pepper

This is a traditional dressing for Niçoise Salad (page 146) but is also excellent with green salads and bean salads.

Method: Whisk all the ingredients together.

Avocado and Kiwi Salsa ◆VEGAN◆

1 avocado, peeled and cut into cubes

1 kiwi fruit, peeled and diced into little cubes

2 spring onions, finely sliced

1 tbsp fresh coriander, chopped

1/2 lime, juiced

1 tsp apple juice concentrate

This salsa goes well with Creole Rice and Beans (page 121).

Method: Mix everything together and eat at once, as the avocado will discolour if left.

Salsa Verde ◆VEGAN◆

2 garlic cloves, peeled

50 g fresh mint, destalked

25 g fresh basil, destalked

1/2 bunch watercress, de-stalked

1 tbsp apple juice concentrate

1 tbsp white wine vinegar

125 ml extra virgin olive oil

Serve with Sweet Romano Peppers (page 78), Griddled Asparagus (page 163), roasted vegetables or simply as a sauce for pasta.

Method: Put everything in the food processor in the order given in the ingredients list, whizzing each time before adding the next ingredient. The mix should be runny, add more olive oil if it starts to get too thick.

Herb and Yoghurt Raita ◆VEGAN◆

125 g soya yoghurt

50 ml soya cream

plenty of fresh mint and coriander, finely chopped

salt and freshly ground black pepper

Serve with Cajun Beefy Tomatoes (page 108) and Roasted Acorn Squash (page 162).

Method: Mix all ingredients together and chill.

Vegan yoghurt is made in exactly the same way as milk yoghurt, but using soya milk.

Cucumber Chutney ◆VEGAN◆

3 garlic cloves, chopped

1 green chilli, chopped

1/2 green pepper, chopped

2 tbsps fresh mint, chopped

1/2 cucumber, roughly chopped

1 tsp apple juice concentrate

1 lime, juiced

pinch of salt

Serve with Sweet Potato Puri and Spicy Indian Roast Vegetables (page 122).

Method: In a food processor purée the garlic and chilli, add the green pepper and mint and whiz. Add the cucumber and whiz again, maintaining the chunky quality.

Stir in the apple juice concentrate, lime juice and salt.

Basil Pesto ◆VEGAN◆

75 g pinenuts, toasted
75 g hazelnuts, roasted, and skins rubbed off
3 garlic cloves, peeled
75 g fresh basil
175 ml olive oil
2 tbsps lemon juice
1 tbsp white wine vinegar
1 tbsp apple juice concentrate
salt and freshly ground black pepper

Serve with bruschetta or spread on bagels and tortilias. See the Lebanese Wrap (page 42).

Method: In a food processor or pestle and mortar, grind the pinenuts and hazelnuts roughly and then decant them into a bowl and set aside.

Purée the garlic in a little of the olive oil, then add the basil and the rest of the olive oil and purée just enough to break up the basil.

Add the lemon juice, apple juice concentrate and vinegar and blend quickly.

Pour the basil and garlic mixture into the ground nuts and stir in.

Vegan Sour Cream ◆VEGAN◆

4 tbsps vegan yoghurt
2 tbsps vegan cream
1 tsp lemon juice
chopped fresh chives
freshly ground black pepper.

Serve with the Trio of Ginger Roasted Squash (page 164).

Method: Simply mix all the ingredients together and chill.

Thai Red Curry Paste ◆VEGAN◆

8 dried red chillies
10 black peppercorns
1 tbsp whole coriander, dry roasted
1 tsp ground cardamom
1 tsp salt
1 onion, chopped
6 large red chillies, sliced
4 tbsps chopped coriander root
4 tbsps chopped lemon grass
2 tbsps chopped garlic
2 tbsps lime zest
1 tbsp fresh galangal
2 tbsps vegetable oil

The essential ingredient for Thai Red Curry (page 129)

Method: Grind the dried chillies, peppercorns, coriander, cardamom and salt in a spice mill. Mash the onion, red chillies, coriander root, lemon grass, garlic, lime zest, galangal and oil in a mortar or in the food processor.

Mix the wet and the dry ingredients together to make a smooth red paste.

Refrigerate half the mix and freeze the rest in measured amounts of about 2 tablespoons for future use.

GLOSSARY OF INGREDIENTS

Ajowan: Ajowan (or carom) seeds are from the caraway family and have a strong thyme-like flavour.

Apple juice concentrate: Made from pure apple juice with no added sugar. Use instead of sugar or honey to sweeten both sweet and savoury dishes. After opening keep in the fridge.

Asafoetida powder: Asafoetida powder, also known as 'hing', is derived from resin from the root or stem of the asafoetida plant grown in Afghanistan. Often used in Indian cookery as a substitute for garlic, when garlic is not allowed for religious reasons. Before cooking it has such an odorous smell its nick name is 'devil's dung'. Asafoetida aids digestion and relieves colic in babies.

Balsamic vinegar: A highly fragrant, sweetish vinegar from Modena in northern Italy. Balsamic vinegar is made from concentrated grape juice and the must from Trebbiano grapes, and is aged in a succession of different woods for at least 10 years. Balsamic vinegar is great with strawberries and black pepper.

Brinjal: This is the Indian name for aubergine. Baby brinjal are wonderfully sweet and tender and about 8 cm long. I have only been able to buy them from Asian stores.

Chillies: Generally the smaller the size the more powerful the heat kick. Red chillies are not necessarily hotter than green, as red chillies are ripe and tend to be sweeter. The hottest part of the chilli is the white membrane, called the capsaicin, which holds the seeds. The seeds are the next hottest. For a milder flavour scrape out the membrane and the seeds.

Be very careful preparing chillies as there is nothing worse than chilli oil in the eyes, wash your hands really well with soapy water before touching any sensitive parts.

Clarified butter or ghee: Ghee is butter that has been heated up and strained to remove the impurities that cause butter to burn and go rancid. In hot countries clarified butter keeps better and does not need refrigerating. Butter ghee is very high in cholesterol. We use a vegan version of ghee made from vegetable oil. The Taj Mahal brand is available from wholefood shops and Indian stores.

Coconut: Coconut milk is the liquid extracted from the grated flesh of the coconut after soaking it in hot water. Coconut cream is thickest coconut milk from the first pressing. Creamed coconut is made from compressed coconut cream.

Cornmeal: White, yellow, or rarely blue, cornmeal is made from dried maize (corn) kernels ground to varying degrees of fineness.

Couscous: Couscous is made from durum wheat grains, which are steamed, dried and cracked. Durum wheat is grown throughout the Mediterranean and is also used for making pasta and semolina. Couscous is the staple carbohydrate of North Africa.

Crème fraîche: A thickened, slightly sour cream, which is delicious in savoury and sweet dishes.

Curry leaves: Curry leaves are the leaves from a native Indian tree, they give off a spicy aroma when rubbed. Try and buy fresh curry leaves as they are much more pungent than dried. Keep fresh curry leaves in the freezer in a sealed bag. Use in Indian curries.

Curry leaves are not related to curry powder. Curry powder is made up of a variety of ground spices.

Dolcelatte: Dolcelatte means 'sweet milk' in Italian. It is a soft, creamy, mild, blue-veined Italian cheese made from cows' milk.

Feta: is a Greek white, crumbly, salty cheese, made from cows', ewes' or goats' milk cut into small blocks. Its name comes from 'fetes', which is the Greek word for a block.

Filo pastry: Filo is paper-thin pastry sheets made from wheat flour and water. Filo pastry is difficult to make so buy it ready made.

Galangal: Galangal is a rhizome (underground stem) from the ginger family. It is a lovely pale pink colour and has a subtle perfumed smell. It has a much more delicate flavour than ginger and is always used in Thai cooking. Buy it from Asian stores. Galangal does not store well, so use it quickly or freeze it in small pieces. To use peel and chop finely.

Ginger: Ginger is native to Southern Asia and it is the rhizome that we eat. To make ginger juice, grate a thumb sized piece of fresh ginger with the skin on, take the ginger into the palm of your hand and squeeze the juice into a marinade. Ginger is from the same family as turmeric and galangal.

Gluten: Gluten is the name given to the proteins in wheat. In baking it is the gluten in the flour which gives the dough its elasticity, resulting in a light, soft loaf. Bread is made with wheat flour with a high gluten content, often called strong flour. Bread made with gluten-free flours is always dense and crumbly. Gluten can be extracted from bread dough by washing the dough under running water. The starch is rinsed off leaving a spongy mass, which is called seitan. (See seitan)

Gluten-free flours: Rice flour, gram flour and all bean flours, soya flour, potato flour, buckwheat flour and corn or maize flour.

Gram flour: Gram flour, sometimes called besan flour (Indian), is ground chickpea flour. It is excellent for batters and has the added advantage of being gluten-free.

Green papaya: Green papaya has the texture of a firm marrow, but with much lower water content. Green papayas are only available from Asian stores.

Green peppercorns: Green peppercorns are soft green under-ripe peppercorns. You can buy them fresh in Asian stores or jarred, preserved in brine, from supermarkets. Fresh are best as they are lovely and crunchy. If you use green peppercorns in a jar make sure you rinse off the brine.

Haloumi: Haloumi is a Middle Eastern semi-hard white cheese made from ewes', goats' or cows' milk. It has a salty, lactic flavour similar to feta and is often flavoured with mint. Haloumi is excellent grilled on barbecues as it does not melt or crumble.

Hoisin sauce: Hoisin sauce is a thick brown sauce made from soya bean paste, garlic, vinegar, sugar and spices. Buy hoisin sauce ready made in jars from Asian stores and supermarkets.

Jaggery: Jaggery or palm sugar is traditional Indian brown sugar made from the sap of the palmyra palm. It is sold in round cakes or cylinders, is very hard, but is easy to grate and has a flavour similar to molasses, but not as overpowering. You can buy jaggery from Asian stores. Alternatively use a mixture of dark brown and light brown soft sugar.

Kecap manis: Kecap manis is a sweet, dark soya sauce from Indonesia. You can buy it from oriental stores and in the specialist section of some supermarkets. If you can't find any mix 2 tablespoons of shoyu with 1 teaspoon of brown sugar.

Lemongrass: Lemongrass is the fresh or dried stalk and leaves of a perennial grass native to south Asia. It is commonly used in Thai cooking. To prepare lemongrass, cut off the dry top $1/3$, peel off the outer layer and slice very finely.

Lime leaves: Lime leaves come from the makrut (kaffir) lime. Fresh lime leaves are very pungent, they keep well in the freezer, but must be kept in an airtight container otherwise everything in the freezer will be imbued with lime aroma.

Linseeds: are the seeds of the flax plant and are rich in essential fatty acids. Black linseeds are traditionally added to bread. Golden linseeds are delicious gently roasted and sprinkled on salads.

Mango: A rain forest fruit with hundreds of different types. My favourite are the small yellow-skinned varieties from India. These are perfumed, sweet and succulent and come individually wrapped in tissue paper and packed in colourful boxes. They are only available from Asian stores. Green mangoes are unripe and are the essential ingredient for mango chutney.

Mascarpone: Mascarpone is a slightly sour full-fat Italian cheese.

Mirin: Mirin is Japanese sweet rice wine exclusively for cooking. You can substitute a well flavoured sweet sherry, but it has rather too strong a flavour.

Miso: Fermented soya beans and grains (wheat, barley or rice) are left to mature and gradually darken in colour from cream, through red, to brown, finally becoming a dark brown salty paste tasting rather like soya sauce. Used as a flavouring and condiment, it is a very good source of B vitamins.

Mitsuna: The young leaves are slightly bitter and are used in salad mixes.

MUSHROOMS

Chestnut: A brown topped button mushroom but with a nutty flavour. Quite often available organically grown.

Oyster: An edible wild mushroom with a short stalk on one side of the smooth bare oyster-like cap which can be up to 15 cm in diameter. It grows on the trunks of deciduous trees and has a rather tough, chewy, juicy flesh with no smell but a slightly fishy flavour.

Porcini/Ceps: Porcini are found during October growing wild in wooded areas in both southern France and Italy. Along with truffles, porcini have never been successfully cultivated and are therefore always expensive.

Widely available dried, the best are pale in colour and are more expensive than the darker brown ones. Soak for 30 minutes in warm water to re-hydrate and then slice thinly. Dried porcini have a concentrated flavour so you don't need many to flavour a dish. They are delicious added to a risotto.

To cook fresh porcini, clean off any dirt and keep the stems as they are just as delicious as the rest. Slice thickly and fry or char grill. Drizzle with the best olive oil, flavour with chopped garlic or fresh parsley or serve with shavings of hard goats' cheese and toasted walnuts.

Portobello/Portobella Mushrooms (*Agaricus bisporus*): Portobello mushrooms are a cultivated mushroom similar to the wild field mushroom. They are nutty brown in colour with a flat cap and can grow up to 12 cm in diameter. They have a firm texture, so are ideal for stuffing and barbecuing.

Shiitake: The Japanese name for this dark brown tough mushroom with a meaty flavour. Shiitake mushrooms grow on dead tree logs and are readily available fresh.

NOODLES

Noodles are made from a mixture of flour and water formed into long ribbons similar to pasta. There are many types.

Egg noodles: Egg noodles are made with wheat flour and egg.

Bean thread, glass or cellophane noodles: Bean thread, glass or cellophane noodles are made with bean flour and water. They are transparent and gluten-free.

Rice noodles: Rice noodles are made with rice flour and water and are gluten-free.

Japanese noodles: Japanese noodles or ramen are either made from wheat and called udon or somen, or made from buckwheat and called soba.

OILS

Olive: Extra virgin olive oil is always cold-pressed and the olives are pressed mechanically without the use of solvents. Extra virgin olive oil must have 1% or less oleic acid, the less oleic acid the better the quality. Tastes vary from sweet and fruity to bitter and almondy to green and peppery. Similar to wine, the finest olive oil is made by single estates and varies from year to year and from estate to estate. Single estate olive oil is the most expensive. Use extra virgin for salad dressings, marinades and Mediterranean dishes where the strong flavour will enhance the dish.

For cooking and frying I prefer to use a lighter olive oil with a higher oleic content and a milder flavour.

Sunflower or soya: Sunflower and soya oils have a neutral flavour and are ideal for everyday use and in Indian and Far Eastern dishes.

Sesame, toasted: Toasted sesame oil has a strong nutty flavour and should be used sparingly in Far Eastern dishes, adding it just at the end of the cooking. Keep sesame oil in the fridge or it will go rancid.

Hazelnut/Walnut/Pumpkin: These oils are excellent for pepping up salad dressings. Keep in the fridge.

Peanut or Groundnut/Rapeseed/Corn: These oils are good for deep-frying as they all have a high smoke point, enabling you to push temperatures higher before the oil burns. The knack for crisp deep-frying is to have a high oil temperature so that the food is sealed at once and doesn't soak up the oil.

Coconut: Coconut oil is the most commonly used oil in Indonesia and is the cheapest. It has an overpowering sickly flavour that permeates anything that it is cooked with. It is also the unhealthiest oil to use and is best avoided.

Pak Choy: Pak choy tastes similar to Swiss chard with a slightly mustard taste. Choose small very fresh looking pak choy with bright green leaves and creamy stems.

Paneer: Paneer is traditional Indian cheese, made from curds acidified with lemon juice. Raw, it has a rubbery tasteless quality, but when cooked it absorbs the cooking flavours, doesn't melt and is solid enough to hold together. Available from Asian stores.

Parmesan: Twineham Grange Farm make the best vegetarian Parmesan. It is made in the traditional Italian way but with English milk and vegetarian rennet. For vegan Parmesan, try Parmazano made by Florentino.

Passata: Passata is made from thick puréed tomatoes. Ideal for soups and sauces when you want a smooth texture. You can buy passata in cartons or jars. After opening keep in the fridge and use up in a few days.

Polenta: Polenta is the staple carbohydrate of northern Italy and is made from fine yellow maize/corn meal. It is very bland on its own, but can be enriched with butter, olive oil, cheese or herbs. The consistency can vary from soft, like mashed potato, to firm for grilling.

Traditional polenta takes about 45 minutes of vigorous stirring to cook. 'Easy cook' polenta, which has already been part-cooked, takes only five minutes. It may not have quite the flavour of traditional polenta, but is much gentler on the biceps.

Pomegranate seeds: Pomegranate seeds are from the sour pomegranate. They are dried and have a lovely ruby colour and a sweet and sour flavour. They are also known as anardana.

Poppadoms: Poppadoms are made from lentil flour and are vegan and gluten-free. Buy them rather than make them. The best way to cook poppadoms is to fry them in a little oil. Alternatively you can grill them, brushing them first with oil. My favourite variety is black pepper. They also come in garlic, chilli and plain.

Pink peppercorns: These are not actually peppercorns but are the aromatic dried red berries of a tree, Schinus Molle. They have a brittle outer shell enclosing a small pepper-like seed.

Punch puran: Punch puran is an Indian spice mix of cumin seeds, coriander seeds, cardamom, black pepper and cloves. You can buy it from Asian stores.

Puy lentils: Puy lentils are small and greenish-brown. They are the most expensive of the lentils and are thought of as a delicacy in France.

Quinoa: Quinoa is a tiny golden seed from South America. Cultivated since 3000 BC, it has higher protein content than rice and is gluten-free.

Rampi: Rampi is a long green palm-like leaf. Also known as pandanus or screw pine, it is used for flavouring in Malay, Thai and south Indian food.

RICE

Basmati rice: A long grain slender rice with a nutty flavour. The best basmati rice is grown in the foothills of the Himalayas.

Paella rice: Spanish paella rice is not as starchy as risotto rice and is the best for paella. It is grown in Valencia. Paella rice should be fluffy and the grains separate.

Black rice: Black rice is shiny black glutinous rice native to Indonesia where it is more commonly used in sweet rice pudding. You can buy it from Asian stores.

Jasmine rice: Jasmine fragrant rice is aromatic long grain rice with a subtler flavour than basmati. It is also called Thai fragrant rice.

Risotto rice: The most popular risotto rice is Arborio rice, a medium grain starchy rice grown in northern Italy.

Wild rice: Wild rice is not actually rice, but the seed from a rush plant *Zizania aquatica*, which grows wild in the Great Lakes of North America. It is now cultivated in the Far East. It has always been very expensive, as the seeds have been traditionally gathered in the wild. The seeds are shiny ebony black and have a nutty flavour.

Rice wine vinegar: Made by fermenting a cooked ground rice mash, rice wine vinegar has a sherry-like taste. Clear and amber coloured varieties are available.

Rocket: Also called arugula, rocket has slightly bitter, peppery dandelion shaped leaves. It is delicious in salads.

Saffron: Saffron threads are the red/orange three branched styles of the crocus and is grown from the Mediterranean to the mountains of Kashmir.

Saffron has to be picked by hand, making it the most expensive spice in the world. It colours food a brilliant gold, is very aromatic, verging on the medicinal, and should be used sparingly.

Make sure you buy the threads, usually sold in tiny clear plastic boxes, as powdered saffron is often not pure.

Sake: Sake is Japanese rice wine, brewed from steamed rice and the mould *Asperigillus oryzae*. You can substitute it with dry white wine.

SEAWEED

Edible seaweeds, which may be green (shallow water), brown, or red (deep water) are usually dried. There are lots of different varieties:

Laver seaweed: Laver seaweed is from west Wales and is made into laver bread.

Dulse: Dulse is purple in colour and is native to Ireland. It is delicious dry-roasted.

Nori: Nori comes in sheets, for making sushi rolls. Make sure you buy toasted nori.

Hiziki and Arame: Both come finely shredded, have a mild flavour and are essential to miso soups.

Carrageen: Carrageen is used as a natural thickener.

Agar agar: Agar agar is derived from seaweed and is a vegetarian setting agent and alternative to gelatine.

Seitan: Seitan is wheat gluten, it is vegan and very high in protein. The best, tastiest seitan is a brand called Yakso, which comes in a jar, marinated in flavoured tamari. It's only available in wholefood shops.

If you can't get marinated seitan, then the alternative is tinned, sometimes called 'mock duck', which is rather oily and even has fake duck skin! Drain off the oil and rinse before using.

Shaoxing rice wine: Shaoxing rice wine is the most famous Chinese rice wine. It is made from fermented glutinous rice, is amber in colour and softer in taste than sherry.

Shoyu: A naturally fermented soya sauce made from soya beans, wheat, salt and water.

Sichuan pepper: Sichuan pepper is a Chinese spice made from the berries of a native ash tree; it has a spicy, mouth numbing taste and adds a kick to curries in a similar way to chillies. It is the most important ingredient in 5-spice mix.

Soya milk: Soya milk is made from soya beans and is vegan and gluten-free. It is high in protein, low in fat and free from cholesterol.

Soya milk can be used as a substitute for cows' milk in soups, sauces, quiches, puddings and milk shakes. Unfortunately it always curdles in coffee.

Soya cream: Use soya cream as a substitute for dairy cream.

Soya yoghurt: Try to find Yofu, which is now readily available in wholefood shops and supermarkets.

Squash, butternut: A bulbous, pear shaped, pale yellow, winter squash with orange flesh.

Suet, vegetarian: Vegetable suet is now easy to find in wholefood shops and supermarkets.

Sweet chilli sauce: Sweet chilli sauce is available in small bottles from supermarkets, but if you get addicted to it, large absurdly good value bottles are available from Asian stores.

Sweet potato: No relation to the white potato, there are two types, one with white flesh, crisp and chestnut-like and one with orange flesh that is sweet and floury.

Tamari: A naturally fermented dark, strong soya sauce made from soya beans, salt and water. Tamari is gluten-free and about twice as strong as shoyu.

Tamarind: Has a sour flavour with a sweet aftertaste. In South East Asia and India it is used in the same way as lemon juice to sour and to bring out the flavour in food. Tamarind paste is extracted from the pods of the tropical tree *Tamarindus indica*.

You can buy tamarind in blocks, which look rather like squashed dates. To extract the pulp, break off a chunk from the tamarind block, cover with just enough hot water and leave to soak. Then squeeze out the pulp and discard the fibre and seeds.

You can also buy tamarind concentrate which is much stronger than tamarind pulp, so you only need to use a little.

Elephants have a predilection for large balls of tamarind pulp.

Tempeh: Tempeh comes from Indonesia and is made of compressed lightly fermented soya beans. Packed full of protein, it is free from cholesterol and has a delicious nutty flavour and chewy texture.

Tempeh is made from soya beans that are soaked, deskinned, split and steamed until tender. The culture *Rhizopus oligosporus* is then added and the beans are packed in banana leaves, or now more commonly perforated plastic bags, and left to mature. As the tempeh matures it develops a darker colour with black streaks and a rich yeasty flavour. The black streaks are natural, akin to the veins in blue cheese.

You can only buy tempeh frozen from wholefood shops and Asian stores. Keep in the freezer.

Teriyaki sauce: Teriyaki sauce is a rich, sweet Japanese sauce made from sake, mirin, tamari and sugar. You can buy it ready made, but it is easy to make and homemade tastes much better.

Thai basil: Thai basil, sometimes called holy basil, has a darker leaf than sweet basil and a sharper, more aromatic flavour. Thai basil is easy to grow or can be bought from Asian stores. As an alternative use sweet basil with some fresh mint added.

Tofu/Soya bean curd: Tofu is an amazing food, which has yet to be taken full advantage of in the West. It is very versatile and can be easily transformed into a myriad of delicious protein-rich dishes. As it has no discernible taste you can infuse it with whatever flavour you like.

Tofu is highly nutritious and an excellent substitute for meat, fish and dairy products. For vegetarians it is a valuable source of protein. Tofu is low in calories, very low in saturated fat, free of cholesterol, high in calcium (often lacking in a dairy-free diet) and a good source of B vitamins and iron.

Tofu is ready to use straight from the packet, it can be used in savoury and sweet dishes, eaten hot or cold, be marinated, deep-fried, pan-fried, baked, grilled, casseroled, puréed and stuffed.

Taste and texture is up to you, it depends on your choice of marinade and method of cooking. The most common types of tofu are firm, smoked and silken.

Firm tofu is standard tofu, easy to cut into cubes, it will keep its shape for stir-frying and deep-frying. Once opened keep in the fridge covered in water, changing the water daily. Use within 4 days.

Smoked tofu has a smoky flavour and is delicious served cold in a salad.

Silken tofu is very smooth and soft and is ideal for puddings, dips and sauces, but is not suitable for stir-frying.

Tofu is made from soya beans, which are soaked for 10 hours then ground, mixed with water into a mash and drained through muslin to produce soya milk. The soya milk is then boiled with a setting agent/coagulant, in China calcium sulphate (natural gypsum) or in Japan nigari (bittern) a by-product from making salt. In the same way as making soft cheese, the whey is drained off leaving the solid tofu.

Tortilla: A thin pancake made from maize flour or wheat flour, shaped and flattened by hand and cooked on both sides on a griddle until dry. Can be filled, wrapped or rolled as tacos, wraps or enchiladas. Not to be confused with Spanish tortillas, which are omelettes.

Umeboshi: Umeboshi plums are actually Japanese apricots, coloured red with shiso leaves and pickled in salt. Umeboshi has a salty flavour and is served at the end of a meal to aid digestion. It is also used in cooking.

Vanilla pod: The fruit of the vanilla vine, used to flavour desserts. To make vanilla sugar, place a couple of vanilla pods in a jar of caster sugar and the sugar will take up the flavour of the vanilla.

Vanilla extract/essence: Make sure that you buy a pure vanilla extract as the cheap vanilla essences are made with synthetic vanillin, which tastes very artificial.

Vegetable bouillon powder: I prefer vegetable bouillon powder to stock cubes. Bouillon powder has a more delicate flavour, is easier to measure out and can be dissolved directly into a dish. Choose a low salt vegan variety. My favoured brand is Marigold.

Wasabi: A Japanese condiment paste with a luminous bright green colour. It is also known as Japanese horseradish. Even though it is not related to horseradish it does have a similar fiery flavour and can bring tears to the eyes! Wasabi is usually eaten as a condiment with sushi.

MEASUREMENTS

All the measurements in this book are metric and the oven temperatures are given in centigrade and Gas Mark.

Millilitres to Fluid Ounces

25 ml = 1 fl oz

50 ml = 2 fl oz

75 ml = 3 fl oz

100 ml = 4 fl oz

150 ml = 5 fl oz

Millilitres to Pints

275 ml = $\frac{1}{2}$ pint

425 ml = $\frac{3}{4}$ pint

570 ml = 1 pint

1 litre = $1\frac{3}{4}$ pints

1150 ml = 2 pints

Centigrade to Gas Mark

110°C = Gas $\frac{1}{4}$

130°C = Gas $\frac{1}{2}$

140°C = Gas 1

150°C = Gas 2

170°C = Gas 3

180°C = Gas 4

190°C = Gas 5

200°C = Gas 6

220°C = Gas 7

230°C = Gas 8

240°C = Gas 9

American Equivalents

1 ml = $\frac{1}{5}$ teaspoon

5 ml = 1 teaspoon

15 ml = 1 tablespoon

34 ml = 1 fluid oz

100 ml = 3.4 fluid oz

240 ml = 1 cup

1 litre = 34 fluid oz

1 litre = 4.2 cups

1 gram = .035 ounce

100 grams = 3.5 ounces

1 kilogram = 2.205 pounds

16 tablespoons = 1 cup

5 tablespoons + 1 teaspoon = $\frac{1}{3}$ cup

2 tablespoons = $\frac{1}{8}$ cup

1 tablespoon = $\frac{1}{16}$ cup

2 cups = 1 pint

2 pints = 1 quart

3 teaspoons = 1 tablespoon

48 teaspoons = 1 cup

EQUIPMENT

You need very little equipment to cook with, to get started all you need is a good sharp knife, a chopping board, a wok and a wooden spoon.

Knives

You need just three knives; a large chef's knife, a small all purpose knife and a serrated bread knife.

Good chef's knives are expensive, but if you look after them they should last for years. The choice of knife is up to you. It's best to try out different makes. Go for one which feels comfortable in your hand, with a good grip and a strong blade that is not flexible. Keep your knife in a knife block, so that the tip doesn't get bent. Sharpen them little and often but get into the habit of sharpening your knife every time you use it.

Knife sharpener

I use a table Chantry knife sharpener, which you can fix to a work surface. It's very easy to use, just pull your knife through the steels a few times before use.

For Japanese global knives you will need to use a wet stone as the global knife has to be sharpened at an angle.

Chopping board

I like to use a thick wooden board that is heavy enough not to move around on the work surface. The best way to preserve your wooden board is to wipe it down after using and then gently oil it with a drop of olive oil. If you have a plastic chopping board lay a damp cloth underneath it to stop it slipping when chopping.

Wok

I use a traditional Chinese wok made from carbon steel. They are cheap and will last a long time if looked after. When you buy your new wok it will be coated in a protective oil, which needs to be scrubbed off before use. The wok then needs to be 'seasoned', which involves burning on thin layers of oil to give it a black, non-stick coating.

To season a new wok; heat the wok and then swirl round a tablespoon of oil. Let this burn on for 5 minutes, then rub off with kitchen paper and repeat until the inside of the wok is black all over.

To keep this seasoned surface, just wipe out your wok after use and brush with oil. If food sticks to the wok, use a wok brush to clean it, never use an abrasive sponge or detergent. Before putting your wok away, always dry it and brush it with oil. Store the wok in a dry place, if it gets wet it will go rusty.

For occasional use a non-stick wok is fine, but these tend to be thicker than steel and not such good conductors of heat.

For electric ovens and Agas you can buy flat-bottomed woks.

Saucepans

My favourite saucepans are solid, heavy stainless steel ones. The most important factor in a successful saucepan is a thick base which lessens the chance of food burning. There is nothing more infuriating than rice catching on the bottom of the saucepan, onions burning before they are cooked or the crème Anglaise turning to scrambled egg. Thick-based saucepans tend to be more expensive but they are worth the extra expense.

Steamer

A small metal steamer/saucepan is invaluable. Make sure that it is quite tall so that you can steam asparagus and sweetcorn. I use a steamer for all leafy vegetables. This has the added benefit that there is no need to strain them, just lift off the steamer and put the vegetables straight into a serving bowl.

Non-stick frying pan

A non-stick frying pan with sloping sides is great for omelettes, pancakes, dry-frying haloumi and anything which could stick.

Blender

If I had to choose between a blender and a food processor, I would go for the food processor, as it is more versatile. Blenders come into their own when smoothness is the essence. They are great for soups, sauces, fruit smoothies and milk shakes. Robust blenders will also crush ice.

Food processor

Food processors can chop, grate, mix, whip and knead. They are the ultimate in labour saving. Their only drawbacks are the cleaning involved and the storage of a bulky machine. I use my food processor mostly for making salsas and for whipping cream and egg whites.

Electric hand held blender

An electric hand held blender is great for whipping cream and egg whites and making fruit smoothies. They are easy to clean and cheap to buy.

Mini food processor

Mini food processors have now become popular, ideal for whizzing up small quantities of baby food and for finely chopping garlic, chillies and root ginger.

Coffee/Spice grinder

Good for grinding freshly roasted spices. It's best to keep one specially for spices, otherwise your spices are tainted by coffee or your coffee tainted by spices. After use just wipe out with a piece of dry kitchen paper.

Scales

Scales are essential for accurate measuring. I like electronic scales, which can measure dry and wet ingredients and convert from ounces to grams.

Set of measuring spoons

You can buy a neat set of stainless measuring spoons in sizes ranging from $1/4$ teaspoon to a tablespoon.

1 teaspoon = 5 mls

1 tablespoon = 15 mls

TECHNIQUES

Ginger juice

Grate the ginger root with the skin on, on the largest side of your grater. Then scoop the grated ginger into the palm of your hand and squeeze the juice into a bowl.

Peeling tomatoes

Make a small slit in each tomato and place them in a heatproof bowl. Pour on boiling water and leave for 5 minutes. Take the tomatoes out of the water and peel off the skins.

Preparing mangoes

The easiest way to peel a mango is to stand the mango upright with the narrow side towards you and slice down each side a little way from the stalk, as the stone is large and flat sided. To eat, score each mango cheek with a knife in a grid pattern, but don't slice through the skin. Fold back the skin and the mango cubes pop up and are easy to either slice off or just suck!

Roasting peppers

Cut the peppers in half lengthways and remove the seeds and core. Cover a baking sheet with silver foil. Place the peppers on the baking sheet, rounded side up.

Place under a hot grill and roast until the tops of the peppers turn brown and begin to char. Remove the peppers from under the grill and put them in a bowl. Cover the top of the bowl tightly with clingfilm and leave the peppers for 20 minutes to sweat and cool.

When the peppers are cool peel off the charred skin.

Zesting

Cover your zester/grater with a piece of baking parchment, so that you rub the citrus fruit against the baking parchment which will collect all the zest. When you have finished zesting, peel off the baking parchment and scrape the zest into the bowl. Much easier and less wasteful than using a knife to clean the zest out of the zester.

Stir-frying

Preparation is the key to a successful stir-fry.

Make sure you have everything ready before you heat the wok. Have your vegetables sliced in individual bowls, the sauce prepared and the rice or noodles cooked.

Heat the wok and add just a tablespoon of oil, heat the oil and then start adding your vegetables. Start with the hardest vegetables, such as carrots, stir-fry quickly over the hottest heat you can, lifting the wok up if the vegetables begin to burn. Continue adding different vegetables, quickly stir-frying and sealing them before adding the next variety. Add liquid near the end of the stir-frying.

Add shoyu and salt right at the end, otherwise the salt will make the vegetables exude their juices and the result will be mushy.

The stir-frying only takes a few minutes and you need to serve the stir-fry as soon as the vegetables are just tender, but still with a crisp bite, a few minutes too long and the vegetables will loose their vibrant colour and go soft.

Deep-frying

The safest way to deep-fry at home is with a small domestic deep-fat fryer, as the heat is controlled and the high sides of the fryer prevent the hot oil splattering.

Otherwise use a wok, its rounded shape means that it heats up quickly and you use less oil. Fill the wok ½ full with rape seed, sunflower or pure vegetable oil. Heat, testing when the oil is ready with a chunk of bread. When the bread floats to the top and bubbles the oil is ready to use. The knack for crisp deep-frying is to have a high oil temperature so that the food is sealed at once and doesn't soak up the oil.

Gently put in the food a few pieces at a time with a perforated ladle. Use the perforated ladle to scoop out the fried food and drain on kitchen paper.

To prevent the oil splattering, make sure that the food is as dry as possible, for example with marinated tofu, pat the tofu dry with kitchen paper before frying. Make sure the food is well sealed, for example momo should be well sealed so they do not fall apart in the fryer.

Cooking rice

For long grain rice, basmati or Thai fragrant rice, rinse well, place in a saucepan, add cold water up to a finger knuckle, approx 2 cm above the rice, cover with a tight fitting lid, bring to the boil and boil for one minute. Turn off the heat and leave to stand with the lid on for 10 minutes, then just fork through and serve at once.

Cooking pasta

Whether you choose to use fresh or dried pasta, the cooking method is the same. You need to start with a large saucepan of salted boiling water. Add a tablespoon of olive oil to stop the pasta sticking together. Bring to the boil and add the pasta. Fresh pasta takes about 3–5 minutes to cook, dried pasta 10–12 minutes. Drain the pasta when it still has a bite to it and serve at once.

Shallow-frying

Shallow-frying is an easier alternative to deep-frying. You have to turn the food so that it fries evenly and you tend not to get as crisp a result as with deep-frying.

Dry roasting

Dry roasting brings out the flavour in spices. Heat a small frying pan without any oil and add the spices. Keep on stirring until they begin to smoke and smell fragrant. Decant at once onto a plate, as they will continuc to cook in the frying pan and burn easily.

Dry roast spices separately as they cook at different times, for example cumin seeds roast twice as quickly as coriander seeds.

Grinding

Grind spices either with a pestle and mortar or in a coffee grinder. It's best to have a coffee grinder just for spices.

INDEX

Thanks

It's been 15 years since we opened Demuths and many people have worked with us both. A great number have become close personal friends.

Thanks to all those chefs, waiting staff, washers up, both past and present. All those who contributed recipes, ideas and advice some of which we didn't understand the significance of till maybe later.

Special thanks to the insuperable Guy, Charlotte, Kelley, Sita, Phil, Claire W, Lucy B, Emma W, Mari who have all worked their pants off and played hard. We've had fun!

To Glynis who has had such patience designing this book with us, Alice and Caroline for their proofing, Mark for all of his photography, and especially Jan for her artistic flair and food styling.

And to all of those thousands of people who have given us their support by eating at Demuths, many, many times over for, without all of you we wouldn't have a business, they wouldn't have a job, we wouldn't have had such fun and at times heartache. But, come to think of it, you wouldn't have had such great food without all of us.

Eat well. Be positive. Be well.

Rachel and Nicho 2002